Table Of Contents

Section 7: Integrations and Extensions

Section 8: Best Practices and Pitfalls to Avoid

Section 9: Case Studies and Real-World Applications

Section 10: Future-Proofing Your Skills

Appendices

- Appendix A: Glossary of Monday.com Terms and Features
- Appendix B: Quick Reference Guide for Keyboard Shortcuts
- Appendix C: Template Library for Common Project Types
- Appendix D: Resources for Continued Learning

~ Conclusion

Disclaimer

This book is an independent resource and is not officially affiliated with, endorsed by, or sponsored by any company, organization, or trademark holder referenced within. All trademarks, service marks, product names, and company names or logos mentioned are the property of their respective owners. Use of these names or terms is solely for identification and reference purposes, and no association or endorsement by the respective trademark holder is implied. The content of this book is based on publicly available information, the author's research, and personal insights. This book is intended for educational and informational purposes only.

Welcome & What You'll Learn

Welcome to *Monday.com for Project Managers: Blueprint to Success*

Project management has evolved significantly over the years, and in today's digital landscape, efficiency and collaboration are more crucial than ever. Whether you're managing a small team or overseeing a complex, multi-department project, having the right tools at your disposal can make all the difference. That's where *Monday.com* comes in.

This book is designed specifically for project managers who want to master Monday.com to streamline workflows, enhance team collaboration, and drive project success. Whether you're new to the platform or looking to optimize your existing workflows, this guide will serve as your blueprint for success.

Why This Book Matters

There are countless project management tools available today, but Monday.com stands out because of its flexibility, ease of use, and robust set of features. Many teams adopt the platform but struggle to fully harness its potential. This book was created to help you avoid common pitfalls and unlock the true power of Monday.com.

By the end of this book, you'll be able to:

- Confidently navigate the Monday.com interface and set up workspaces tailored to your needs.
- Build effective workflows that align with your team's goals and project requirements.
- Leverage automations, integrations, and reporting tools to improve productivity.
- Foster seamless team collaboration and communication within the platform.
- Avoid common mistakes and implement best practices to maximize efficiency.

Who This Book Is For

This book is for project managers at all levels—whether you're a beginner trying to set up your first board or an experienced professional looking to refine your workflow. If you're a:

- **Project Manager** seeking a better way to oversee tasks, deadlines, and team progress.
- **Team Leader** looking to improve collaboration and accountability among team members.
- **Business Owner** aiming to streamline operations and project execution.
- **Freelancer or Consultant** managing multiple clients and projects at once.
- **Monday.com User** wanting to take your skills to the next level.

No prior experience with Monday.com is required—this book will take you from the basics to advanced techniques, step by step.

How This Book Is Structured

To ensure a smooth learning experience, this book is divided into ten structured sections:

- **Section 1: Introduction to Monday.com for Project Managers** – Understand why Monday.com is a powerful tool for project managers and how it fits into modern workflows.

- **Section 2: Getting Started with Monday.com** – Learn how to create an account, set up your workspace, and navigate the platform with ease.
- **Section 3: Core Features of Monday.com** – Dive deep into boards, columns, groups, dashboards, and visual tools that help you manage projects efficiently.
- **Section 4: Building Your Project Management Workflow** – Discover how to set up a project board, assign tasks, track progress, and automate repetitive workflows.
- **Section 5: Collaboration and Team Dynamics** – Master team collaboration features, including file sharing, comments, and integrations with communication tools.
- **Section 6: Advanced Techniques for Project Success** – Explore automations, time tracking, workload management, and advanced filtering for data insights.
- **Section 7: Integrations and Extensions** – Learn how to connect Monday.com with third-party apps like Google Drive, Slack, and CRM tools.
- **Section 8: Best Practices and Pitfalls to Avoid** – Get expert advice on optimizing Monday.com, avoiding common mistakes, and scaling workflows for larger teams.
- **Section 9: Case Studies and Real-World Applications** – See how real teams use Monday.com for agile project management, marketing, and remote collaboration.
- **Section 10: Future-Proofing Your Skills** – Stay ahead by learning about new features, industry trends, and career growth strategies with Monday.com.

Additionally, the book includes appendices with a glossary, keyboard shortcuts, and ready-to-use templates to help you implement what you've learned.

How to Get the Most Out of This Book

To ensure you get the maximum benefit from this guide, follow these tips:

- **Follow Along Practically** – As you read, try applying what you learn directly within your Monday.com account. Hands-on practice will solidify your understanding.
- **Use the Checklists and Tips** – Each section includes actionable insights to help you implement best practices effectively.
- **Refer Back as Needed** – This book is structured as both a learning guide and a reference manual. Feel free to revisit sections as you encounter new challenges.
- **Experiment and Customize** – Monday.com is highly flexible, so don't be afraid to tweak features and workflows to match your unique project needs.

Let's Get Started!

You're about to embark on a journey that will transform the way you manage projects. Whether you're tackling tight deadlines, coordinating across teams, or simply looking to improve efficiency, this book will help you navigate Monday.com with confidence.

Let's dive in and unlock the full potential of Monday.com for project management!

Section 1:
Introduction to Monday.com for Project Managers

Preface: Why This Book Matters

Project management has evolved significantly in the last decade. Traditional methodologies, manual tracking, and disconnected communication tools have given way to digital platforms that promote automation, efficiency, and collaboration. In this fast-paced environment, project managers are expected to juggle multiple projects, streamline workflows, and ensure team productivity—all while staying agile in response to changing priorities.

Monday.com has emerged as a powerful tool in this new era, providing a centralized, intuitive, and flexible solution to modern project management challenges. However, many users only scratch the surface of what Monday.com can truly offer. That's where this book comes in.

Why This Book?

With countless project management tools available today, why focus on Monday.com? Simply put, it stands out due to its:

- **Customizability** – It adapts to diverse industries, project types, and team structures.
- **User-Friendly Interface** – Designed for ease of use without compromising on functionality.
- **Automation and Integrations** – Saves time by reducing manual work and connecting with other business tools.
- **Collaborative Features** – Encourages transparency, accountability, and seamless team communication.
- **Scalability** – Whether you're a freelancer or managing enterprise-level operations, Monday.com grows with you.

Despite its strengths, new users often struggle to unlock the full potential of the platform. Without the right guidance, it's easy to feel overwhelmed by its numerous features, settings, and customization options. That's why this book was created—to provide project managers with a structured, easy-to-follow blueprint to mastering Monday.com.

What You'll Gain from This Book

By the end of this book, you will:

- **Master the Monday.com Ecosystem** – Learn how to navigate the platform, customize workspaces, and utilize key features effectively.
- **Build Efficient Workflows** – Set up boards, automate repetitive tasks, and integrate external tools for a seamless workflow.
- **Enhance Team Collaboration** – Use real-time collaboration features, manage permissions, and facilitate smooth communication.

- **Boost Productivity and Accountability** – Leverage dashboards, reports, and time-tracking tools to measure performance and meet deadlines.
- **Avoid Common Mistakes** – Learn best practices and pitfalls to ensure a smoother implementation and adoption process.

Who This Book Is For

This book is for:

- **Project Managers** – Looking to improve team coordination and workflow efficiency.
- **Team Leaders** – Managing multiple projects and ensuring team accountability.
- **Business Owners** – Seeking a scalable project management solution for operations.
- **Freelancers and Consultants** – Organizing multiple clients and projects in one system.
- **Monday.com Users** – Wanting to go beyond the basics and fully utilize the platform.

Whether you're new to Monday.com or looking to optimize your current setup, this book will provide actionable insights tailored to your needs.

How to Use This Book

To make the most of this guide:

1. **Follow Along Step-by-Step** – Apply concepts practically within your Monday.com account as you read.
2. **Use the Actionable Tips** – Each chapter includes best practices and key takeaways for easier implementation.
3. **Refer Back When Needed** – This book serves as both a learning guide and a reference manual for ongoing use.
4. **Experiment and Adapt** – Customize features to suit your specific industry, team, and project needs.

A Tool That Grows With You

Project management is not one-size-fits-all, and neither is Monday.com. As your team, projects, and responsibilities evolve, this platform will continue to adapt alongside you. This book will equip you with the knowledge and confidence to leverage Monday.com for immediate success while preparing for future challenges and opportunities.

Now, let's dive into the Monday.com ecosystem and explore how this platform can revolutionize the way you manage projects.

Understanding the Monday.com Ecosystem

In today's fast-paced work environment, managing projects effectively requires more than just to-do lists and email threads. Project managers must juggle multiple moving parts—tasks, timelines, teams, and resources—all while ensuring seamless collaboration and real-time updates.

Monday.com is designed to simplify this complexity. It provides a **centralized, visual, and highly customizable platform** that empowers teams to manage workflows, automate repetitive tasks, and enhance productivity. Whether you're overseeing a small project or handling enterprise-level operations, Monday.com adapts to your needs.

To fully leverage Monday.com, it's essential to understand its core components and how they fit together. This chapter provides an overview of the Monday.com ecosystem, its key features, and why it's such a powerful tool for project managers.

The Core Components of Monday.com

At its core, Monday.com is structured around a few key elements that define how information is organized and managed:

1. Workspaces: Organizing Your Projects at a High Level

A **Workspace** is the top-level structure where you organize your projects, teams, and workflows. Think of it as a digital headquarters that houses everything related to your work. Within a workspace, you can create multiple boards, dashboards, and folders to manage different projects efficiently.

- **Use Case Example:** A marketing agency might have separate workspaces for different clients, each containing its own set of project boards and workflows.

2. Boards: The Foundation of Work Management

Boards are where the actual project management happens. A **board** is a visual representation of a project, process, or workflow. Each board consists of **groups, items, and columns**, allowing teams to organize tasks, track progress, and collaborate seamlessly.

- **Types of Boards:**
  - **Main Boards** – Visible to everyone in the workspace.
  - **Private Boards** – Restricted to selected team members.
  - **Shareable Boards** – Can be shared with external stakeholders.

3. Groups: Structuring Tasks and Milestones

Inside a board, **groups** help organize items into logical sections. These could represent different phases of a project, priority levels, or categories of work.

- **Use Case Example:** In a product launch project, groups might include **"Planning,"** **"Development," "Marketing," and "Launch."**

4. Items: The Actionable Tasks

Items (also called tasks or rows) represent individual tasks, action items, or deliverables. Each item can have its own set of attributes, including assigned team members, due dates, status updates, and dependencies.

- **Use Case Example:** In a software development sprint, an item might be **"Develop Login Feature,"** assigned to a developer with a due date and priority label.

5. Columns: Structuring Data Effectively

Columns define the type of information stored within each item. Monday.com provides a variety of column types to suit different project needs, such as:

- **Status Columns** – Track progress (e.g., "To Do," "In Progress," "Completed").
- **Timeline Columns** – Manage deadlines and project schedules.
- **People Columns** – Assign tasks to team members.
- **Numbers & Formula Columns** – Track budgets, hours worked, or other numerical values.

By combining different column types, you can create highly customized workflows tailored to your team's requirements.

Beyond the Basics: Enhancing Workflow with Monday.com Features

Understanding the foundational elements of Monday.com is just the beginning. The platform's real power lies in its **automation, integrations, and data visualization capabilities**.

1. Automations: Reducing Manual Work

Monday.com allows users to set up **rules-based automations** that trigger specific actions when conditions are met. Automations can help reduce repetitive tasks, such as:

- Automatically moving tasks to "In Progress" when assigned to a team member.
- Sending reminders before deadlines approach.
- Notifying stakeholders when a task is completed.

2. Integrations: Connecting with Other Tools

Monday.com integrates with a wide range of third-party applications, making it easy to **sync data, streamline communication, and enhance productivity.** Some key integrations include:

- **Slack & Microsoft Teams** – For team communication.
- **Google Drive & Dropbox** – For document storage and sharing.
- **Zoom** – For seamless video conferencing.
- **CRM Tools (Salesforce, HubSpot)** – For managing sales and customer interactions.

These integrations eliminate the need to switch between multiple apps, keeping everything centralized within Monday.com.

3. Dashboards: Gaining Insights at a Glance

Dashboards provide **real-time visual insights** into project progress, team workloads, and key performance metrics. You can customize dashboards with widgets such as:

- **Progress Tracking** – Monitor completed vs. pending tasks.
- **Time Tracking** – Measure time spent on tasks.
- **Workload Management** – Balance workloads across team members.

With dashboards, project managers can make **data-driven decisions** without digging through multiple boards manually.

Why Monday.com is Ideal for Project Managers

Monday.com stands out as a **flexible, scalable, and user-friendly** platform for project management. Here's why it's a game-changer for teams:

- **Customizable Workflows:** Unlike rigid project management tools, Monday.com adapts to your preferred workflow rather than forcing you into a predefined structure.
- **Collaboration-Centric:** Its built-in communication features (comments, mentions, and updates) ensure that teams stay aligned.
- **Scalability:** Whether you're managing a **small startup or a global enterprise**, Monday.com grows with your needs.
- **User-Friendly Interface:** Even those new to project management tools can quickly get up to speed without extensive training.

As we move through this book, you'll learn how to **leverage these features effectively**, ensuring that you're not just using Monday.com—but truly optimizing it for maximum project success.

What's Next?

Now that you have a foundational understanding of the Monday.com ecosystem, the next chapter will explore why it's considered a **game-changer for project managers.** You'll discover how its unique approach to **workflow automation, collaboration, and customization** makes it a standout tool in the world of project management.

Why Monday.com is a Game-Changer for Project Managers

Project managers today are expected to do more than just oversee tasks and deadlines. They must balance team collaboration, optimize workflows, manage risks, and drive results—all while keeping stakeholders informed. Traditional project management tools often fall short in addressing these demands, leading to inefficiencies, communication gaps, and missed deadlines.

Monday.com changes the game by providing **a dynamic, intuitive, and highly customizable** platform that empowers project managers to:

- **Plan, track, and execute projects seamlessly**
- **Automate repetitive tasks to boost efficiency**
- **Enhance collaboration with real-time communication tools**
- **Integrate with essential business applications**
- **Gain actionable insights through advanced reporting and dashboards**

This chapter explores the key reasons why Monday.com stands out as a **must-have** tool for modern project managers.

1. A Fully Customizable Project Management Solution

One of the biggest challenges with traditional project management tools is their **rigid structure**—forcing teams to adapt their workflows to fit the software rather than the other way around. Monday.com flips this model by offering **total flexibility** to design workflows, track progress, and organize projects in a way that makes sense for your team.

- You can create **custom boards** tailored to any project type—whether you're managing a marketing campaign, a software development sprint, or a client project.
- With **dozens of column types**, including status, priority, timeline, numbers, and formulas, you can track the exact data points you need.
- **Views like Kanban, Gantt, and Calendar** ensure that every team member can work in a format that best suits their needs.

This level of customization ensures that **Monday.com adapts to you**, rather than forcing you into a pre-defined workflow.

2. Powerful Automation to Reduce Manual Work

Time-consuming manual tasks are one of the biggest obstacles to productivity. Monday.com helps project managers eliminate repetitive work with **built-in automation features**, enabling teams to focus on higher-value tasks.

With **no coding required**, you can set up automations that:

- Move tasks to "In Progress" when a team member is assigned.
- Send deadline reminders to team members and stakeholders.
- Automatically update statuses when dependencies are met.
- Notify project leads when urgent issues arise.

By automating repetitive tasks, Monday.com helps teams **save hours of work each week**, ensuring that no important updates or deadlines fall through the cracks.

---

3. Seamless Team Collaboration & Communication

Effective project management relies on **clear communication**. Monday.com ensures that team members stay aligned with real-time collaboration tools that eliminate the need for long email threads and constant status meetings.

- **Task Comments & Mentions** – Every task (item) has a built-in comment section where teams can discuss details, share updates, and tag colleagues for quick responses.
- **Live Status Updates** – Team members can update progress in real time, ensuring that everyone has the latest information.
- **File Sharing & Document Management** – Upload, attach, and preview documents directly within Monday.com, keeping project assets easily accessible.
- **Integration with Slack, Zoom, and Microsoft Teams** – Keep communications centralized and ensure that key updates are shared across platforms.

These features make Monday.com a **one-stop collaboration hub**, reducing friction and ensuring that teams stay informed and productive.

---

4. Real-Time Dashboards & Reporting for Data-Driven Decisions

Project managers need access to **real-time data** to make informed decisions. Monday.com provides **powerful dashboards and reports** that help you:

- Track project progress at a glance.
- Monitor team workloads to prevent burnout.
- Measure key performance indicators (KPIs).
- Identify bottlenecks and areas for improvement.

Dashboards can be fully customized with widgets such as:

- **Progress Trackers** – Visualize task completion rates.
- **Workload Distribution** – Ensure a balanced team workload.
- **Time Tracking Reports** – Monitor time spent on tasks.
- **Budget and Resource Allocation** – Keep financials on track.

These insights **empower project managers** to proactively address challenges, optimize workflows, and drive success.

---

5. Integration with Essential Business Tools

Most project managers rely on multiple tools to handle communication, file sharing, and data management. Monday.com seamlessly integrates with **over 40+ essential business applications**, allowing teams to centralize their workflows without switching between different platforms.

Popular integrations include:

- **Google Workspace & Microsoft 365** – Sync with Calendar, Drive, and Outlook.
- **Slack & Microsoft Teams** – Get real-time project updates in your communication tools.

- **Zoom** – Schedule and launch meetings directly from Monday.com.
- **Jira & Trello** – Sync tasks between development and project teams.
- **CRM Tools (Salesforce, HubSpot)** – Align sales and project management teams.

By connecting with existing business applications, Monday.com eliminates silos and enhances workflow efficiency.

---

6. Scalability for Teams of Any Size

Whether you're managing a **small team or a large enterprise**, Monday.com grows with your needs.

- **Startups & Small Teams** – Use Monday.com to keep projects organized and team members aligned.
- **Mid-Sized Companies** – Scale operations with automation, integrations, and custom workflows.
- **Large Enterprises** – Manage complex workflows, compliance needs, and multi-department projects seamlessly.

With **enterprise-grade security, permissions, and compliance features**, Monday.com ensures that your data remains **secure and accessible only to authorized users**.

---

7. User-Friendly Interface with Minimal Learning Curve

Many project management tools require extensive training before teams can use them effectively. Monday.com, however, is designed for **intuitive use**.

- **Drag-and-drop functionality** makes updating tasks and workflows simple.
- **Pre-built templates** allow teams to get started quickly.
- **Custom views and filters** enable users to focus on the most relevant data.

Even users with **no prior project management experience** can quickly get up to speed, reducing onboarding time and maximizing productivity.

Why Monday.com is the Future of Project Management

With **customizable workflows, automation, real-time collaboration, and powerful reporting**, Monday.com is **more than just a project management tool—it's a complete work operating system.**

Project managers who embrace Monday.com can expect to:

- Reduce administrative workload and manual tracking
- Improve team communication and accountability
- Optimize project timelines and resource allocation
- Enhance decision-making with real-time data insights
- Adapt workflows to evolving project needs

Whether you're **leading a small team or managing enterprise-wide operations**, Monday.com provides the **scalability, efficiency, and flexibility** needed to drive success.

What's Next?

Now that you understand why Monday.com is a **game-changer for project managers**, it's time to get started. In the next chapter, we'll walk you through **creating your Monday.com account** and setting up your first workspace.

Let's dive in and put these insights into action!

Section 2:
Getting Started with Monday.com

Creating Your Monday.com Account

Before you can take full advantage of Monday.com's powerful project management features, you need to create an account and set up your workspace. Whether you're a solo project manager or part of a large team, the signup process is quick and straightforward. This chapter will guide you through creating your Monday.com account, setting up your workspace, and configuring your first board so you can start managing projects right away.

Step 1: Signing Up for Monday.com

To create a Monday.com account, follow these steps:

1. **Go to the Monday.com Website**
   - Open your preferred web browser and navigate to [www.monday.com] (https://www.monday.com).
   - Click on the **"Get Started"** or **"Sign Up"** button.
2. **Choose Your Sign-Up Method**
   Monday.com offers multiple sign-up options:
   - **Email Sign-Up** – Enter your work email and click **"Continue."**
   - **Google Account Sign-Up** – If you use Google for work, you can sign up instantly with your Google credentials.
   - **Microsoft Account Sign-Up** – Teams using Microsoft 365 can connect directly.
3. **Verify Your Email**
   - Monday.com will send a verification email to the address you provided.
   - Open the email and click on the verification link to confirm your account.
4. **Enter Basic Information**
   After verification, you will be prompted to:
   - Enter your **full name**
   - Create a **password** (if not using Google or Microsoft sign-in)
   - Provide your **company name** (optional)

Step 2: Setting Up Your Workspace

Once your account is created, Monday.com will guide you through setting up your workspace. A **workspace** is where all your boards, tasks, and projects will live.

Choosing a Workspace Type

Monday.com will ask how you plan to use the platform. You can select from options such as:
- **Project Management** (Ideal for structured team workflows)
- **Marketing & Creative** (Best for campaign tracking and content planning)
- **Sales & CRM** (For tracking leads and customer relationships)

■ **Software Development** (Agile sprints, bug tracking, and dev roadmaps)
■ **HR & Recruiting** (Candidate tracking and team onboarding)

If you're unsure, select **"Project Management"**—you can customize your setup later.

Inviting Team Members (Optional)

Monday.com will prompt you to invite colleagues to your workspace. You can:

- **Enter team members' email addresses** to send invitations.
- **Skip this step** if you want to set up your workspace first before inviting others.

Step 3: Customizing Your First Board

After setting up your workspace, you'll be directed to create your first **board**—the foundation of project management in Monday.com.

Using a Template or Starting from Scratch

Monday.com offers pre-built templates tailored for different use cases. Some useful templates for project managers include:

- **Project Tracker** – For managing tasks, deadlines, and team responsibilities.
- **Sprint Planning** – Designed for Agile workflows.
- **Marketing Campaign** – To oversee promotional activities and deadlines.
- **Event Planning** – For scheduling and coordinating events.

If you prefer a customized setup, choose **"Start from Scratch."**

Naming Your Board

Give your board a meaningful name based on your project or team. Examples:

- **Website Development Roadmap**
- **Client Onboarding Workflow**
- **Product Launch Plan**

Selecting a Board Type

- **Main Board** – Visible to everyone in your workspace.
- **Private Board** – Restricted to selected team members.
- **Shareable Board** – Can be shared with external collaborators (clients, vendors, etc.).

For most project managers, a **Main Board** is a good starting point.

Step 4: Understanding Your Dashboard and Features

After setting up your first board, you'll land on your **Monday.com dashboard**, where you can start managing projects. Key areas include:

1. **Navigation Panel (Left Sidebar)**
   - **Workspaces:** Organize boards by team, department, or function.
   - **Boards:** Your active projects and workflows.
   - **Inbox:** Centralized notifications for updates, mentions, and task changes.

- Search & Filters: Quickly find tasks, team members, and files.
2. Your First Board Layout
    - Groups: Sections within a board for organizing tasks (e.g., "To-Do," "In Progress," "Completed").
    - Items (Tasks): Actionable tasks assigned to team members.
    - Columns: Custom fields such as status, priority, deadline, and assigned person.

Step 5: Setting Up Your Profile and Notifications

To personalize your Monday.com experience, update your profile settings:

- **Click on your profile picture (top right corner).**
- **Edit your name, job title, and profile picture** for easy identification.
- **Configure notifications** (email, in-app, or desktop) to stay informed about project updates.

What's Next?

Congratulations! You've successfully created your Monday.com account, set up your first workspace, and built your first board. Now, it's time to **dive deeper into the platform**.

Navigating the Dashboard: A Walkthrough

The **Monday.com dashboard** is the heart of your project management experience. It's where you **access boards, track progress, manage tasks, and collaborate with your team in real-time**. Whether you're leading a small team or overseeing multiple projects, knowing how to navigate the dashboard efficiently will help you **stay organized, streamline workflows, and improve team productivity**.

In this chapter, we'll take a step-by-step walkthrough of the **Monday.com dashboard**, exploring its key components and functionalities so you can confidently manage projects from day one.

The Main Dashboard Layout

When you log into Monday.com, you'll land on the **main dashboard interface**. The dashboard consists of several key sections:

1. The Left-Side Navigation Panel (Primary Control Center)

The **left sidebar** is your main navigation tool. It provides quick access to:

- **Workspaces** – Organize your projects, teams, and tasks efficiently.
- **Boards** – Your active project management boards where tasks and workflows live.
- **Inbox** – View notifications and updates from team members.
- **My Work** – A centralized view of your assigned tasks across all boards.
- **Dashboards** – Visualize project progress, workload distribution, and key metrics.
- **Apps & Integrations** – Connect third-party tools like Slack, Google Drive, and Zoom.
- **Search Everything** – Quickly find tasks, documents, or team members across all workspaces.

💡 **Tip:** You can collapse or expand the sidebar by clicking the small **arrow icon** at the bottom of the panel, giving you more screen space when needed.

2. Workspaces: Structuring Your Projects

A **Workspace** acts as a container for all your boards and projects. It helps you organize tasks by **team, department, or function**.

For example:

- A **marketing team** might have workspaces for **Campaign Planning, Content Production, and Social Media Management**.
- A **software development team** could have workspaces for **Sprint Planning, Bug Tracking, and Feature Requests**.

Within each **workspace**, you can create **multiple boards** to manage specific projects or workflows.

💡 **Tip:** If you're working across multiple teams, you can **switch between workspaces** using the **drop-down menu** in the left navigation panel.

3. Boards: The Core of Task Management

Boards are where all your project management activities happen. Each board consists of:

- **Groups** – Sections within a board (e.g., "To-Do," "In Progress," "Completed").

- **Items (Tasks)** – Individual tasks or action items.
- **Columns** – Custom fields such as priority, due dates, task owner, and progress status.

You can create three types of boards:

■ **Main Boards** – Visible to everyone in your workspace.
■ **Private Boards** – Restricted to selected team members.
■ **Shareable Boards** – Can be shared with external stakeholders, such as clients or vendors.

💡 **Tip:** You can **switch between different board views (Kanban, Gantt, Timeline, Calendar, etc.)** using the **View button** at the top of the board.

---

4. My Work: Your Personalized Task Center

The **My Work** section is your personal productivity hub. It provides a **centralized view of all tasks assigned to you across multiple boards**.

In this section, you can:

- **Filter tasks by due date, status, or priority.**
- **Sort tasks based on different time frames** (Today, This Week, Next Week).
- **Mark tasks as completed directly from the list.**

💡 **Tip:** If you manage multiple projects, check **My Work daily** to **prioritize** your tasks effectively.

---

5. Inbox: Real-Time Updates & Notifications

The **Inbox** keeps you informed of all activity within your workspace. It's where you receive:

- **Mentions (@yourname) from team members.**
- **Task updates and status changes.**
- **Automation-triggered notifications (e.g., "Task Due Tomorrow").**

💡 **Tip:** Click the **"Mark as Read"** option to clear notifications after reviewing updates.

---

6. Dashboards: Project Tracking & Reporting

Dashboards in Monday.com allow you to **visualize project data** in real-time. You can create a dashboard to track:

■ **Project Progress** – Monitor task completion rates.
■ **Team Workload** – Ensure work is evenly distributed.
■ **Time Tracking** – Analyze how much time is spent on tasks.
■ **Budget & Resource Allocation** – Keep financials in check.

Dashboards can be customized using **widgets**, such as:

■ **Pie Charts** – Display task distribution.
■ **Timeline View** – Track project deadlines.
■ **Calendar View** – View upcoming due dates.

💡 **Tip:** Dashboards are **especially useful for project managers and executives** who need a high-level overview of multiple projects.

---

7. Search & Filter: Finding What You Need Quickly

The **Search Everything** feature (found in the left sidebar) allows you to locate:

🔍 **Tasks, boards, team members, and documents.**
🔍 **Conversations within task comments.**
🔍 **Files uploaded to different boards.**

💡 **Tip:** Use **advanced filters** (by date, status, or assignee) to narrow down search results.

Quick Actions for Efficient Navigation

Now that you know where everything is, here are **some quick actions** to boost your efficiency:

◾ **Create a New Task Quickly** – Click the "+ Add" button at the top of any board.
◾ **Change a Task Status** – Click on the task's status column and update it (e.g., "To Do" → "In Progress").
◾ **Mention a Team Member** – Use **@username** in the task comments to notify them instantly.
◾ **Set Due Date Alerts** – Enable **deadline reminders** in the task settings.
◾ **Switch Between Board Views** – Use **Timeline, Kanban, or Calendar** views for better visualization.

What's Next?

Now that you're familiar with the **Monday.com dashboard**, you're ready to **start customizing your workspace** to fit your project management needs.

Let's move forward and start building a project management system that works for you!

Customizing Your Workspace for Project Management

A **well-structured workspace** is essential for efficient project management. Monday.com provides a **highly customizable** environment, allowing you to tailor your workspace to match your team's unique workflows, processes, and priorities. Whether you're managing a marketing campaign, a software development sprint, or an internal operations project, optimizing your workspace ensures **clarity, productivity, and accountability**.

In this chapter, we'll cover how to:
- Set up workspaces and boards for different projects.
- Customize columns, groups, and items for task tracking.
- Optimize views for improved visualization and efficiency.
- Use folders and permissions for better organization and security.

By the end, you'll have a **personalized project management system** that aligns with your team's workflow.

Step 1: Structuring Your Workspaces

Monday.com allows you to **create multiple workspaces** to manage different projects, departments, or teams. A **workspace** is like a digital headquarters where all related boards, dashboards, and automations live.

How to Create and Name Workspaces

1. Click on **"Workspaces"** in the left sidebar.
2. Select **"+ Add Workspace"** and enter a name.
3. Choose a **visibility setting**:
    - **Main** (accessible to all team members).
    - **Private** (restricted to selected members).
    - **Shareable** (collaborate with external clients or vendors).

Best Practices for Organizing Workspaces

- **For multiple teams**: Create workspaces by **department** (e.g., "Marketing Team," "Product Development," "Client Services").
- **For multiple projects**: Assign workspaces based on **major projects or clients** (e.g., "Website Redesign," "New Product Launch," "HR Hiring Process").
- **For company-wide management**: Use a **single workspace** and divide projects using **boards and folders**.

💡 **Tip:** Keep workspace names clear and concise for easy navigation.

Step 2: Customizing Boards for Project Tracking

Boards in Monday.com serve as **the foundation of your project management workflow**. Each board is fully customizable, allowing you to track projects **visually and efficiently**.

Choosing the Right Board Type

- **Main Boards**: Used for company-wide collaboration.
- **Private Boards**: Ideal for confidential projects or restricted team access.
- **Shareable Boards**: Best for external collaboration with clients or vendors.

Creating a New Board

1. Click **"+ Add"** in your workspace and select **"Board."**
2. Enter a board name (e.g., "Marketing Roadmap," "Sprint Planning," or "Event Management").
3. Choose whether the board is **Main, Private, or Shareable.**

💡 **Tip:** Start with a **pre-built template** if you need inspiration. Monday.com offers **ready-made project management templates** that can be customized.

Step 3: Customizing Groups, Columns, and Items

Now that you've created a board, it's time to customize its layout.

Using Groups to Organize Tasks

Groups are **sections within a board** that categorize items.
Examples of group structures:

- **Project Phases:** "Planning," "Execution," "Review," "Completed."
- **Task Priority:** "Urgent," "High Priority," "Medium Priority," "Low Priority."
- **Sprints:** "Sprint 1," "Sprint 2," "Sprint 3."

To add a new group:

1. Open your board and click **"+ Add Group."**
2. Rename the group (e.g., "Design Phase" or "Client Approvals").
3. Drag groups up or down to rearrange them.

💡 **Tip:** Use **color-coded groups** to improve visual organization.

Customizing Columns for Better Task Management

Columns define the type of **information** associated with each task. Monday.com offers a variety of column types, including:

Column Type	Purpose
Status Column	Track progress (e.g., "To Do," "In Progress," "Done").
Timeline Column	Manage deadlines and project schedules.
People Column	Assign team members to specific tasks.
Priority Column	Set task importance levels (e.g., High, Medium, Low).
Dropdown Column	Provide multiple-choice options for categorization.

Numbers & Formula Columns	Track budgets, hours worked, or numerical metrics.

To add a column:

1. Click **"+ Add Column"** at the top of your board.
2. Choose a column type from the list.
3. Rename the column and adjust settings.

💡 **Tip: Customize column colors** in the **Status Column** to visually differentiate task stages.

Customizing Items (Tasks) for Better Clarity

Each task (or "item") represents a specific action or deliverable. Customizing task details ensures that **everyone knows what's required**.

How to customize tasks:
- **Click on an item** to open its task card.
- **Add a description** with task objectives.
- **Set due dates and priorities.**
- **Attach files** for easy reference.
- **Use @mentions** to notify team members.

💡 **Tip:** Create **task dependencies** by linking related tasks to ensure proper execution order.

Step 4: Optimizing Board Views for Efficiency

Monday.com provides multiple ways to view your projects based on different **workflow needs**.

View Type	Best For
Table View	Standard list-based project tracking.
Kanban View	Agile workflows and task movement.
Timeline View	Managing deadlines and dependencies.
Calendar View	Visualizing upcoming tasks and due dates.
Gantt Chart View	Long-term project planning and scheduling.

To change views:

1. Open your board and click **"Views" (top-right corner).**
2. Select a view (e.g., Timeline, Kanban, Gantt).
3. Customize the view with filters and sorting options.

💡 **Tip: Use multiple views** to accommodate different team preferences (e.g., Kanban for developers, Gantt for project managers).

Step 5: Using Folders and Permissions for Better Organization

For teams handling multiple projects, **folders and permissions** help keep everything structured.

Organizing with Folders

- Click **"+ Add Folder"** in your workspace.
- Drag and drop **boards into folders** for better categorization.
- Examples of folder structures:
    - **Marketing → Social Media, Content Strategy, SEO Campaigns.**
    - **IT Projects → Software Development, Bug Tracking, Feature Requests.**

Setting User Permissions

Monday.com allows you to control **who can view, edit, or manage** boards.

Permission Type	Functionality
Admin	Full access to modify workspace settings.
Editor	Can edit and update boards.
Viewer	Can view but not edit boards.
Guest	Limited access (for external clients/vendors).

💡 Tip: Use **role-based permissions** to restrict sensitive information from non-essential users.

Final Thoughts

Customizing your workspace ensures that **Monday.com aligns with your team's unique needs**, improving efficiency, collaboration, and clarity.

■ **You've learned how to:**

- Structure workspaces for better organization.
- Customize boards, groups, columns, and tasks.
- Optimize project views for better visualization.
- Use folders and permissions to manage access.

Now that your workspace is set up, it's time to **explore the core features of Monday.com!**

Section 3:
Core Features of Monday.com

Boards: The Foundation of Workflow Management

In Monday.com, **boards are the backbone of project management**. A board is a highly customizable workspace where teams organize, track, and manage tasks, projects, and workflows. Each board consists of **groups, items, and columns**, enabling users to structure their work in a way that best suits their needs.

Whether you're managing a **simple to-do list or a complex multi-phase project**, boards provide the flexibility to keep everything structured, visible, and accessible in real-time.

In this chapter, you'll learn how to:
■ **Create and configure boards for different project needs.**
■ **Customize board layouts using groups, items, and columns.**
■ **Leverage board views to optimize task tracking.**
■ **Use board types (main, private, and shareable) for better collaboration.**

By the end of this chapter, you'll have a **deep understanding of how to use boards efficiently to manage your workflows** in Monday.com.

Step 1: Creating a Board

A board in Monday.com acts as a **centralized hub** for tracking a specific project, team, or workflow. To create one:

1. **Navigate to Your Workspace**
   ○ Open your Monday.com dashboard.
   ○ Click **"+ Add"** and select **"Board"** from the menu.
2. **Name Your Board**
   ○ Choose a descriptive name that reflects its purpose, such as:
      ■ "Marketing Campaign Tracker"
      ■ "Product Development Roadmap"
      ■ "Client Project Management"
3. **Select Board Type**
Monday.com offers three board types, each serving a different purpose:

Board Type	Description	Best Used For
Main Board	Visible to all workspace members.	Internal team projects.

Private Board	Restricted access to selected team members.	Sensitive projects, confidential work.
Shareable Board	Can be shared with external collaborators.	Client projects, vendor partnerships.

💡 **Tip:** If you're collaborating with external stakeholders (clients, freelancers), use **Shareable Boards** for controlled access.

Step 2: Structuring a Board with Groups

Once your board is created, you'll need to **add groups**. Groups are **sections within a board that help categorize and organize tasks**.

Common Ways to Structure Groups

■ **Project Phases:** "Planning," "Execution," "Review," "Completed."
■ **Task Priorities:** "Urgent," "High Priority," "Medium Priority," "Low Priority."
■ **Time-Based Organization:** "Week 1," "Week 2," "Week 3."
■ **Client Management:** "Client A," "Client B," "Client C."

To add a group:

- Click **"+ Add Group"** on your board.
- Enter a name and choose a **color code** for visual distinction.
- Drag and reorder groups as needed.

💡 **Tip:** Use **color coding** to differentiate between phases, priorities, or team ownership.

Step 3: Adding and Customizing Items (Tasks)

Each **task, deliverable, or milestone** within a board is represented as an **item** (or row). Items hold specific details about a project's progress.

How to Add an Item

1. Click **"Add Item"** at the bottom of a group.
2. Name the item (e.g., "Design Homepage Mockups," "Send Client Proposal").
3. Assign owners, set due dates, and update status columns.

💡 **Tip:** Use **@mentions in item comments** to notify specific team members when action is required.

Step 4: Customizing Boards with Columns

Columns allow you to **store and track task details** within a board. Monday.com provides a wide range of **column types**, including:

Column Type	Purpose	Example Use Case
Status Column	Tracks progress stages.	"To Do," "In Progress," "Completed."
Timeline Column	Manages deadlines and schedules.	Tracking a project's duration.
People Column	Assigns team members to tasks.	"John Doe" assigned to "Website Wireframe."
Priority Column	Indicates task urgency.	High, Medium, Low.
Formula Column	Calculates values automatically.	Total project cost, hours worked.
Files Column	Stores attachments related to tasks.	Upload contracts, briefs, or designs.

To add a column:

- Click **"+ Add Column"** at the top of the board.
- Choose the column type and customize settings.

💡 **Tip: Use the "Status Column" to visualize task progress with color-coded indicators** (e.g., Red = "Stuck," Green = "Completed").

Step 5: Exploring Board Views for Enhanced Workflow Management

Monday.com offers multiple **views** to help teams visualize their projects more effectively.

View Type	Best For
Table View	Standard project tracking in rows and columns.
Kanban View	Agile workflows and drag-and-drop task movement.
Timeline View	Managing deadlines, dependencies, and scheduling.
Calendar View	Seeing tasks by due date.
Gantt Chart View	Long-term project planning.

To switch views:

- Click **"Views"** (top-right of the board).
- Select **the desired view** based on your workflow needs.

💡 **Tip:** Use **Kanban View** for Agile project management and **Gantt Chart View** for strategic planning.

Step 6: Managing Board Permissions and Access

To ensure **data security and controlled access**, you can set board permissions for team members.

Permission Type	Access Level
Admin	Full control (create, delete, manage settings).
Editor	Can modify items but cannot change board settings.
Viewer	Read-only access, no edits.
Guest	Limited access for external users (on shareable boards).

To adjust permissions:

- Click **"Board Settings"** > **"Permissions"** > Select access level.

💡 Tip: Set **View-Only access for external stakeholders** to prevent accidental changes to project data.

Step 7: Automating Board Workflows

Automation saves time by reducing **manual work**. You can create **custom automation rules** such as:

■ **Task Status Changes:** "When a task is marked 'Done,' move it to 'Completed' group."
■ **Deadline Reminders:** "Send a Slack message when a task is due in 2 days."
■ **Task Assignments:** "When a new item is added, assign it to [specific team member]."

To set up automation:

- Click **"Automate"** in the board menu.
- Choose from **pre-built automation rules** or **create custom logic**.

💡 Tip: Automate **recurring tasks** to eliminate manual data entry.

Final Thoughts

Boards are the **foundation of workflow management** in Monday.com. By customizing groups, items, columns, and views, you can **create a system that fits your team's workflow perfectly**.

■ **You've learned how to:**

- Create, name, and structure boards.
- Customize groups, items, and columns.
- Use different board views for better visualization.
- Set permissions and automate tasks.

Now that you've mastered boards, the next chapter will **explore columns and data types in more detail**, helping you refine your workflow and optimize task tracking.

Columns and Data Types: Organizing Information Effectively

Monday.com is more than just a simple task management tool—it's a **fully customizable work operating system** that allows project managers to **track, organize, and analyze** information effectively. At the heart of this system are **columns**, which help structure your data in a meaningful way.

Each **board in Monday.com** consists of **groups (sections), items (tasks), and columns**. While **boards and groups** help you categorize tasks, **columns define the type of information** you want to track for each item.

In this chapter, we'll cover:
- **Understanding column types and their use cases.**
- **Choosing the right columns to fit your workflow.**
- **Customizing columns for better data organization.**
- **Using advanced columns for automation and reporting.**

By the end, you'll know how to **optimize your boards with the right column types**, ensuring your projects stay organized, transparent, and efficient.

Step 1: Understanding the Different Column Types

Monday.com offers **over 30 different column types**, but as a project manager, you'll mostly work with a **core set of columns** that help you track tasks, deadlines, and team responsibilities.

Essential Column Types for Project Management

Column Type	Purpose	Example Use Case
Status Column	Tracks progress stages.	"To Do," "In Progress," "Completed."
Text Column	Stores general information.	Task descriptions, meeting notes.
People Column	Assigns team members to tasks.	"John Doe" assigned to "Website Wireframe."
Date Column	Sets deadlines and milestones.	Task due dates, project launch dates.
Priority Column	Defines task urgency.	High, Medium, Low priority levels.
Timeline Column	Displays project schedules.	Visualize task duration over weeks/months.
Files Column	Stores and attaches documents.	Upload contracts, reports, designs.

💡 **Tip:** Use the **Status Column** for quick task tracking and color-code each stage (e.g., **Red = Stuck, Green = Completed**).

Step 2: Choosing the Right Columns for Your Workflow

Each **project type requires a unique combination of columns** to track relevant data. Below are some **common column setups** based on different project management scenarios.

1. Task & Project Management

For general project tracking, include:
- **Status Column** – To track progress.
- **People Column** – To assign tasks.
- **Date Column** – To set deadlines.
- **Priority Column** – To indicate urgency.

2. Agile Sprint Planning & Software Development

For managing **Agile workflows**, include:
- **Status Column** – To track backlog, in-progress, and completed tasks.
- **Timeline Column** – To define sprint duration.
- **Dropdown Column** – To tag specific software features (e.g., UI, Backend).
- **Numbers Column** – To track story points or hours logged.

3. Marketing & Content Planning

For managing campaigns or content schedules, include:
- **Status Column** – To track content stages (Draft, In Review, Published).
- **People Column** – To assign content creators and editors.
- **Date Column** – To track publishing schedules.
- **Files Column** – To store blog drafts, videos, or graphics.

💡 **Tip:** Customize your **board layout** by dragging and reordering columns **based on priority and frequency of use**.

Step 3: Customizing Columns for Better Data Organization

Once you've added the right columns, **customizing them** enhances data tracking and makes it easier for teams to **interpret and act on information**.

1. Renaming Columns for Clarity

Instead of using the default column names, **rename them to better fit your workflow**.
- Instead of "Date," rename it to **"Task Deadline"**
- Instead of "People," rename it to **"Assigned To"**

2. Adjusting Column Width & Order

- Drag and drop columns to rearrange them based on priority.
- Resize columns for better readability.

3. Color Coding for Quick Identification

- Use **custom colors in the Status Column** to make task tracking visually intuitive.
- Example: Green = "Completed," Yellow = "In Progress," Red = "Blocked."

💡 **Tip:** Keep your board **clean and organized** by only adding **necessary columns**—too many columns can clutter your workspace.

Step 4: Using Advanced Columns for Automation & Reporting

Beyond basic tracking, **Monday.com offers advanced columns** to help automate workflows and generate data-driven insights.

1. Formula Column: Automating Calculations

The **Formula Column** allows you to create custom calculations for your project needs.
■ Example: Automatically calculate the **number of days remaining** before a task deadline.

Formula Example:

DAYS({Task Deadline}, TODAY())

This formula calculates how many days remain until a task is due.

2. Mirror Column: Syncing Data Across Boards

The **Mirror Column** pulls data from another board, eliminating duplicate work.
■ Example: Sync a **budget column** from a Finance board into your Project board.

3. Time Tracking Column: Measuring Task Duration

For tracking **time spent on tasks**, use the **Time Tracking Column** to:
■ Start and stop a timer directly from the board.
■ Generate reports on total hours spent per task.

💡 **Tip:** Use the **Formula Column** with **Time Tracking** to calculate total billable hours for a project.

Step 5: Best Practices for Managing Columns Efficiently

To ensure your **Monday.com boards remain efficient**, follow these best practices:

■ **Keep Columns Minimal** – Only use columns that provide valuable data.
■ **Use Consistent Naming** – Standardize column names across different boards.
■ **Leverage Templates** – Save board templates with custom column settings for reuse.
■ **Regularly Review & Optimize Columns** – Remove unused columns to keep boards streamlined.

Final Thoughts

Columns in Monday.com **turn raw data into actionable insights**. By selecting the right columns and customizing them properly, you can:

■ Improve **task tracking and team accountability.**
■ Streamline **workflows with automated data calculations.**
■ Enhance **collaboration by sharing relevant project details.**

Now that you understand how to **organize and track information using columns**, the next chapter will cover **how to structure tasks and subtasks efficiently using groups**.

Groups: Structuring Tasks and Subtasks

In Monday.com, **Groups** are essential for organizing tasks, projects, and workflows efficiently. They serve as **sections within a board** that help categorize work based on different criteria, such as project phases, priority levels, or sprint cycles. Groups allow project managers to **structure work logically, keep teams aligned, and ensure smooth task execution**.

Understanding how to use Groups effectively can help:
- Segment tasks into manageable sections.
- Organize subtasks and dependencies efficiently.
- Enhance team visibility and accountability.
- Improve workflow automation and tracking.

This chapter will walk you through the best ways to **structure and manage Groups** for different project types, ensuring an optimized Monday.com workflow.

Step 1: Understanding the Structure of Groups

A **Monday.com board** consists of **Groups, Items (Tasks), and Columns**:

- **Groups**: High-level categories that organize tasks (e.g., "Planning Phase," "In Progress," "Completed").
- **Items (Tasks)**: Actionable work items within a group.
- **Columns**: Additional details related to each task, such as due dates, status, and ownership.

Groups **serve as containers** for related tasks, ensuring that all work is categorized properly and easy to track.

Step 2: Choosing the Right Group Structure

The way you structure Groups depends on your **project type** and **workflow requirements**. Here are some **common Group structures** to consider:

1. Project-Based Grouping

Useful for **multi-phase projects** that involve different stages of execution.
- **Example Structure:**

  - 🚀 **Planning Phase**
  - 🔧 **Development Phase**
  - 📁 **Testing & Review**
  - ⬛ **Completed**

💡 **Best for:** Software development, product launches, and event planning.

2. Status-Based Grouping

Ideal for **Kanban-style workflows** where tasks move from one stage to another.
- **Example Structure:**

  - 📁 **To Do**
  - 🚀 **In Progress**
  - 🛠 **Under Review**

- ■ Completed

💡 **Best for:** Agile project management, marketing campaigns, and content production.

3. Priority-Based Grouping

Helpful for teams that **prioritize work based on urgency or importance**.
■ **Example Structure:**

- 🔥 **Urgent & High Priority**
- ⌛ **Medium Priority**
- ■ **Low Priority & Completed**

💡 **Best for:** IT support teams, customer service requests, and backlog management.

4. Time-Based Grouping

Works well for teams working in **weekly or sprint-based cycles**.
■ **Example Structure:**

- ■ **Week 1**
- ■ **Week 2**
- ■ **Week 3**
- ■ **Completed Tasks**

💡 **Best for:** Agile teams, social media content planning, and editorial calendars.

5. Team-Based Grouping

Useful for large teams working on different sections of a project.
■ **Example Structure:**

- 🖥 **Development Team**
- 🎨 **Design Team**
- 📣 **Marketing Team**
- 🛠 **Support & Maintenance**

💡 **Best for:** Cross-functional teams, enterprise workflows, and IT operations.

Step 3: Creating and Customizing Groups in Monday.com

To create a new Group:

1. **Open your Board** in Monday.com.
2. Click **"+ Add Group"** at the bottom of your existing groups.
3. **Enter a Name** (e.g., "Sprint 1 Tasks," "High-Priority Issues").
4. **Customize the Color** to differentiate it visually.

💡 **Tip: Use contrasting colors for different Groups** to improve readability and workflow segmentation.

Step 4: Managing Tasks and Subtasks Within Groups

Once Groups are in place, you can start **adding tasks and subtasks**.

Adding Tasks (Items) to a Group

- Click **"Add Item"** under the relevant Group.
- Name the task (e.g., "Design Homepage," "Send Proposal to Client").
- Assign owners, set due dates, and update task statuses.

Using Subtasks for Better Task Breakdown

Subtasks are useful for **breaking down larger tasks into smaller, manageable steps**.

Example:

- **Main Task:** "Launch New Website"
  - ◆ Subtask 1: "Finalize UI design"
  - ◆ Subtask 2: "Develop homepage layout"
  - ◆ Subtask 3: "Test website performance"

Tip: Use the **Subitems feature** to track dependencies and team responsibilities effectively.

Step 5: Enhancing Group Efficiency with Automation

Monday.com allows you to **automate task movements between Groups** to **streamline workflows**.

Common Automations for Groups

Move Completed Tasks Automatically

- **Rule:** "When a task's status changes to 'Completed,' move it to 'Done' Group."

Auto-Assign Team Members Based on Group

- **Rule:** "When a task is added to 'Urgent Issues,' assign it to the Support Team."

Notify Stakeholders Based on Progress

- **Rule:** "When a task moves from 'In Progress' to 'Under Review,' notify the Manager."

Tip: Automating task transitions **reduces manual work and improves efficiency**.

Step 6: Best Practices for Managing Groups in Monday.com

To **keep your Groups organized and effective**, follow these best practices:

Keep Groups Consistent – Use a standard structure across different boards to maintain uniformity.
Limit the Number of Groups – Avoid unnecessary clutter by focusing on key workflow stages.
Use Color Coding – Assign distinct colors to different Groups for easy identification.
Review and Archive Old Groups – Remove or archive Groups that are no longer relevant.
Combine Groups with Board Views – Use Kanban, Timeline, or Calendar views to **visualize Group progress more effectively**.

Tip: Set up a **"Completed Tasks"** Group and archive it monthly to keep your board clean.

Final Thoughts

Groups in Monday.com **create structure and clarity** within your boards, ensuring tasks are organized effectively. Whether you're managing a **sprint, project phases, or team assignments**, properly setting up Groups can **enhance productivity, streamline task management, and improve team collaboration**.

■ **You've learned how to:**

- Choose the right Group structure for different workflows.
- Create, customize, and color-code Groups.
- Organize tasks and subtasks within Groups.
- Automate task movement between Groups.
- Implement best practices for keeping Groups efficient.

Now that you've structured your Groups, the next step is to **optimize task timelines and dependencies** using **Timelines and Gantt Charts**.

Utilizing Timelines and Gantt Charts

Effective project management relies on **clear timelines, task dependencies, and milestone tracking**. Monday.com provides **Timelines and Gantt Charts**, two powerful visual tools that help teams:

■ **Plan projects efficiently** by setting realistic deadlines.
■ **Track task progress** and identify potential delays.
■ **Manage dependencies** to ensure smooth workflow execution.
■ **Optimize resource allocation** by balancing workloads.

This chapter explores how to **utilize the Timeline and Gantt Chart views** in Monday.com, enabling you to **visualize and manage project schedules seamlessly**.

Step 1: Understanding the Difference Between Timelines and Gantt Charts

Both **Timelines and Gantt Charts** are designed to provide a **visual representation of project progress**, but they serve different purposes:

Feature	Timeline View	Gantt Chart View
Purpose	Displays tasks over a period	Shows dependencies, progress, and phases
Best For	Tracking deadlines and schedules	Managing complex projects with dependencies
Flexibility	Focuses on individual task timelines	Provides a structured breakdown of entire projects
Dependencies	Not directly shown	Clearly defined task dependencies

💡 **Tip:** Use **Timeline View** for **simple project tracking** and **Gantt Chart View** for **detailed project planning with dependencies**.

Step 2: Setting Up the Timeline View

The **Timeline View** helps project managers **visualize upcoming tasks, deadlines, and workload distribution**.

How to Add a Timeline View to a Board

1. Open your project board in Monday.com.
2. Click the **"Views"** button in the top-right corner.
3. Select **"Timeline"** from the available view options.
4. Click **"Add to Board"** to save the Timeline View.

How to Configure the Timeline View

■ Assign a **Start Date** and **Due Date** for each task (using a Date Column).
■ Customize colors for different tasks or project phases.

■ Filter tasks by **assignee, priority, or group** for better clarity.
■ Use **drag-and-drop** functionality to adjust timelines quickly.

Tip: If a task needs more time, **drag the task bar to extend the duration** directly in the Timeline View.

Step 3: Using the Gantt Chart View for Advanced Project Planning

The **Gantt Chart View** is an **advanced project planning tool** that includes:
■ **Task dependencies** – Define which tasks must be completed before others start.
■ **Milestones** – Highlight key deadlines and deliverables.
■ **Critical path tracking** – Identify tasks that directly impact the project's deadline.

How to Add a Gantt Chart View to a Board

1. Open your project board.
2. Click **"Views"** > Select **"Gantt"** from the available options.
3. Click **"Add to Board"** to activate the Gantt View.

How to Configure the Gantt Chart

■ Assign tasks **Start Dates, Due Dates, and Dependencies**.
■ Drag tasks to reschedule them in real-time.
■ Enable **Critical Path Mode** to highlight key tasks that affect the project deadline.
■ Adjust task bars to **extend or shorten** the project timeline.

Tip: The **Gantt View automatically updates when task dates change**, ensuring an always-accurate project plan.

Step 4: Managing Dependencies in Gantt Charts

Task dependencies help teams understand **which tasks rely on others before they can be completed**.

How to Set Dependencies in the Gantt View

1. Click on a task in the Gantt View.
2. Select the **"Dependencies"** option.
3. Choose the **preceding task** that must be completed first.
4. The dependency line will appear, connecting related tasks.

Example of Dependencies:

- 🛠 "Complete UI Design" **must be finished before** 🚀 "Develop Front-End Code."
- ✍ "Draft Content" **must be approved before** 📣 "Publish Article."

Tip: Use **dependencies to prevent bottlenecks** by ensuring tasks are completed in the correct order.

Step 5: Using Timelines and Gantt Charts for Resource Management

Monday.com allows you to **balance workloads** and prevent team burnout using Timelines and Gantt Charts.

How to Optimize Resource Management

■ Assign team members to each task using the **People Column**.
■ Use **filters** to see **who is overloaded with tasks**.
■ Reschedule tasks using **drag-and-drop** in the Timeline or Gantt View.

💡 **Tip:** Ensure no team member is overbooked by **limiting task overlap** in the Timeline View.

Step 6: Automating Timeline and Gantt Chart Workflows

Automation can help **streamline project tracking** and **reduce manual updates**.

Common Automations for Timelines & Gantt Charts

■ **Deadline Reminders:** "Send an alert when a task is due in 2 days."
■ **Task Status Updates:** "If a task is overdue, change its status to 'Delayed'."
■ **Project Completion Notifications:** "Notify stakeholders when all tasks in a project are completed."

💡 **Tip:** Automating project tracking ensures **nothing falls through the cracks** and deadlines are met consistently.

Step 7: Best Practices for Using Timelines and Gantt Charts

To maximize efficiency, follow these **best practices**:

■ **Use the Timeline for broad project overviews** and the **Gantt Chart for detailed task dependencies**.
■ **Regularly update deadlines** to reflect project progress.
■ **Color-code tasks** based on urgency, team ownership, or project phase.
■ **Set up dependencies correctly** to avoid scheduling conflicts.
■ **Automate repetitive timeline updates** to reduce manual work.

💡 **Tip:** Review your Timeline and Gantt Chart **weekly** to ensure your project stays on track.

Final Thoughts

Timelines and Gantt Charts in Monday.com provide **powerful visualization tools** that make project tracking and scheduling **seamless and effective**. By using them properly, you can:

■ **Ensure deadlines are met.**
■ **Prevent project bottlenecks.**
■ **Improve team collaboration and workload balance.**
■ **Streamline dependencies and milestone tracking.**

Now that you've learned how to use **Timelines and Gantt Charts**, the next chapter will cover **Dashboards—your go-to tool for real-time project insights and reporting**.

Dashboards: Visualizing Progress at a Glance

Managing projects effectively requires **real-time insights** into progress, deadlines, team workloads, and key performance indicators (KPIs). Monday.com's **Dashboards** provide a **customizable, visual way to track project data**, helping project managers make informed decisions quickly.

With **Dashboards**, you can:
■ **Monitor project progress at a glance.**
■ **Track deadlines and upcoming milestones.**
■ **Analyze team workloads to prevent burnout.**
■ **Visualize KPIs using charts, graphs, and reports.**
■ **Streamline communication by consolidating key metrics.**

This chapter will walk you through how to **create, customize, and optimize dashboards** in Monday.com to gain **valuable insights into your projects and team performance**.

Step 1: Understanding the Role of Dashboards in Monday.com

A **Dashboard** in Monday.com is a **centralized, high-level view of project data** that compiles information from multiple boards into **one visual space**.

Dashboards consist of **Widgets**, which allow you to:

- **Display progress metrics visually** (e.g., Pie Charts, Bar Graphs).
- **Monitor tasks and deadlines** across multiple projects.
- **Track team performance and workloads**.
- **Integrate external data sources** for broader reporting.

💡 **Tip:** Dashboards **do not replace boards**; they **enhance** them by providing an **overview of multiple projects and data points**.

Step 2: Creating a Dashboard

To set up a Dashboard in Monday.com:

1. **Navigate to the Left Sidebar**
   - Click **"+ Add"** and select **"Dashboard"**.
2. **Name Your Dashboard**
   - Choose a relevant name like **"Project Overview," "Team Performance," or "Marketing Campaign Analytics."**
3. **Select Data Sources**
   - Choose the **boards you want to pull data from**.
   - You can select **one or multiple boards** to aggregate data.
4. **Click "Create Dashboard"**
   - Your dashboard will appear as a **blank canvas** ready for customization.

💡 **Tip:** You can **restrict access** to your dashboard by making it **Private, Main, or Shareable**, just like boards.

Step 3: Customizing Your Dashboard with Widgets

Widgets are the **building blocks** of a dashboard. They allow you to **display specific types of information visually**.

1. Essential Widgets for Project Managers

Widget Type	Purpose	Best Use Case
Battery Widget	Tracks project completion percentages.	Monitor progress across multiple boards.
Timeline Widget	Displays project timelines.	Track deadlines and dependencies visually.
Workload Widget	Shows team workload distribution.	Prevent burnout and balance responsibilities.
Chart Widget	Creates pie charts, bar graphs, and line charts.	Analyze KPIs like task completion rates.
Numbers Widget	Displays numerical data dynamically.	Track budgets, hours worked, or total tasks.
Table Widget	Shows board data in a tabular format.	View and manage detailed project insights.
To-Do List Widget	Highlights priority tasks.	Keeps track of outstanding action items.
Countdown Widget	Displays time remaining until a deadline.	Track important project milestones.

💡 **Tip:** Use a **combination of widgets** to create a **balanced dashboard that provides both high-level overviews and detailed insights**.

Step 4: Configuring Key Dashboard Widgets

Let's explore how to **set up the most important widgets** for project tracking.

1. Progress Tracking with the Battery Widget

This widget provides a **real-time status update** on project completion.

- Click **"+ Add Widget" > "Battery"**.
- Select the **Status Column** to track (e.g., "In Progress," "Completed").
- Choose the boards you want to include.

💡 **Tip:** Use color coding (Green = Completed, Yellow = In Progress, Red = Stuck) for better clarity.

---

2. Visualizing Deadlines with the Timeline Widget

The **Timeline Widget** helps you **track multiple projects and deadlines** on a single screen.

- Click **"+ Add Widget" > "Timeline"**.
- Select the **Date Column** to pull deadlines from.
- Adjust the time range (Week, Month, or Year).

💡 **Tip:** Use the **Zoom In/Out** feature to adjust the visibility of short-term and long-term tasks.

---

3. Managing Workloads with the Workload Widget

The **Workload Widget** ensures that **team members are not overloaded with too many tasks**.

- Click **"+ Add Widget" > "Workload"**.
- Select the **People Column** to track task assignments.
- Choose the **Date Column** for deadlines.
- Adjust the capacity per team member (e.g., max tasks per person per week).

💡 **Tip:** Set up **alerts for over-allocated team members** to prevent burnout.

---

4. Tracking KPIs with the Chart Widget

Charts help project managers **analyze trends and performance**.

- Click **"+ Add Widget" > "Chart"**.
- Choose between **Pie, Bar, or Line Graphs**.
- Select the **Status Column** or **Priority Column** to track data.

💡 **Example:**

- **Bar Chart** → Number of tasks completed per team.
- **Pie Chart** → Percentage of tasks by status (To Do, In Progress, Completed).

Step 5: Automating Dashboard Updates

Dashboards in Monday.com **automatically update** when data changes on connected boards. However, you can **enhance automation** with the following:

◼ **Deadline Alerts** – "Notify project lead if a deadline is missed."
◼ **Task Completion Alerts** – "Send an update when 80% of tasks are completed."
◼ **Workload Notifications** – "Alert managers if a team member is overbooked."

💡 **Tip:** Set up **weekly automated reports** to send dashboard summaries via email or Slack.

Step 6: Best Practices for Effective Dashboards

To maximize dashboard effectiveness, follow these **best practices**:

◼ **Keep It Simple** – Use only essential widgets to avoid clutter.
◼ **Use Consistent Colors** – Maintain uniform color schemes for easy readability.
◼ **Update Regularly** – Review dashboard settings weekly to ensure relevance.
◼ **Share with Stakeholders** – Provide access to key stakeholders for transparency.
◼ **Customize for Different Teams** – Create separate dashboards for executives, project managers, and team members.

💡 **Tip:** Use **"Filters" to customize dashboard views** based on team, priority, or project phase.

Final Thoughts

Dashboards in Monday.com **transform raw project data into actionable insights**. Whether you're tracking **task progress, team workloads, or deadlines**, a **well-configured dashboard enhances visibility, accountability, and efficiency**.

■ You've learned how to:

- Create and customize dashboards.
- Use essential widgets for project tracking.
- Automate updates and notifications.
- Implement best practices for dashboard optimization.

Now that you've set up **Dashboards for project tracking**, the next chapter will guide you through **Setting Up Your First Project Board**—the foundation of workflow management in Monday.com.

Section 4:
Building Your Project Management Workflow

Setting Up Your First Project Board

A **well-structured project board** is the foundation of efficient project management in Monday.com. It acts as the central hub where all tasks, deadlines, team assignments, and project milestones are organized. A **clear and well-structured board ensures visibility, accountability, and workflow efficiency**, making it easier for project managers to track progress and optimize team productivity.

In this chapter, you'll learn how to:
■ **Create a new project board from scratch or use a template.**
■ **Structure your board with groups, items, and columns.**
■ **Set up task assignments and statuses for better tracking.**
■ **Use board views to enhance project visualization.**

By the end of this chapter, you'll have a **fully functional project board** that helps you streamline your workflow and manage your team effectively.

Step 1: Creating a New Board

To create a project board in Monday.com, follow these steps:

1. **Go to Your Workspace**
   ○ Open Monday.com and navigate to your workspace.
   ○ Click **"+ Add"** in the left sidebar and select **"New Board"**.
2. **Choose How to Create Your Board**
   ○ **Start from Scratch** – Build a custom board with your own structure.
   ○ **Use a Template** – Select a pre-built project management template from Monday.com.
   ○ **Import from Excel** – Convert an existing project tracker into a Monday.com board.
3. **Name Your Board**
   ○ Pick a descriptive name that clearly defines your project, such as:
      ■ "Website Redesign Project"
      ■ "Marketing Campaign Tracker"
      ■ "Product Launch Timeline"
4. **Select the Board Type**
   ○ **Main Board** – Visible to all team members.
   ○ **Private Board** – Restricted to selected team members for confidential projects.
   ○ **Shareable Board** – Allows external stakeholders (e.g., clients, vendors) to collaborate.
5. **Click "Create Board"**
   ○ Your blank board is now ready for customization.

💡 **Tip:** If you're working with a **remote team or external clients**, use a **Shareable Board** to ensure seamless collaboration while maintaining security.

Step 2: Structuring Your Project Board

Once your board is created, the next step is to **structure it properly**. Monday.com boards consist of:

- **Groups** – Sections that categorize tasks (e.g., "To Do," "In Progress," "Completed").
- **Items (Tasks)** – Individual action items within a group.
- **Columns** – Custom fields that provide additional task details.

1. Adding Groups to Organize Your Board

To add a new group:

1. Click **"+ Add Group"** at the top or bottom of your board.
2. Name the group based on project phases or task priorities, such as:
   ■ **Project Phases:** "Planning," "Execution," "Review," "Completed"
   ■ **Task Priorities:** "High Priority," "Medium Priority," "Low Priority"
   ■ **Time-Based:** "Week 1," "Week 2," "Week 3"

💡 **Tip:** Use **color-coded groups** to visually distinguish different workflow stages.

---

2. Adding Items (Tasks) to Groups

Each item represents a **task, milestone, or deliverable** within the project.

To add an item:

1. Click **"Add Item"** under the relevant group.
2. Enter a **task name** (e.g., "Draft Social Media Plan" or "Develop User Interface").
3. Assign task owners and set deadlines using columns (explained below).

💡 **Tip:** Keep task names **clear and action-oriented** to ensure team members understand their responsibilities.

---

3. Customizing Columns for Task Tracking

Columns define the **type of information** each task should have. Here are the essential columns for project tracking:

Column Type	Purpose	Example Use Case
Status Column	Tracks task progress.	"To Do," "In Progress," "Completed"
People Column	Assigns team members to tasks.	"John Doe" assigned to "Design Logo"
Date Column	Sets deadlines and due dates.	"Task due on March 15"
Priority Column	Defines task urgency.	"High," "Medium," "Low"
Timeline Column	Shows project duration.	"Sprint from Feb 1 - Feb 14"
Files Column	Stores attachments related to tasks.	Upload briefs, designs, or reports

To add a column:

1. Click **"+ Add Column"** at the top of your board.
2. Select the column type that fits your project's needs.

💡 **Tip:** Use the **Formula Column** to calculate task completion rates dynamically.

Step 3: Setting Up Task Assignments and Statuses

Once your board is structured, it's time to **assign tasks** and set up **statuses** for clear progress tracking.

1. Assigning Tasks to Team Members

1. Click on the **People Column** in a task row.
2. Select a **team member** responsible for the task.
3. Ensure workload distribution is balanced using the **Workload View** (covered in later chapters).

💡 **Tip:** Use **@mentions in the task comments** to notify assigned team members of updates.

---

2. Defining Task Statuses for Progress Tracking

The **Status Column** allows you to track progress at a glance.

🔲 **Basic Status Options:**

- ● **To Do** – Task not started.
- ● **In Progress** – Task currently being worked on.
- ● **Completed** – Task finished.

🔲 **Advanced Status Options:**

- ● **Blocked** – Task cannot proceed due to dependencies.
- ● **On Hold** – Task paused temporarily.
- ⚡ **Urgent** – Task needs immediate attention.

💡 **Tip: Automate task status updates** (e.g., "If the task is completed, move it to the 'Completed' group").

Step 4: Enhancing Project Visualization with Board Views

Monday.com allows you to **switch between different views** to visualize projects more effectively.

View Type	Best For
Table View	Standard list-based project tracking.
Kanban View	Agile workflows with drag-and-drop task movement.
Timeline View	Managing deadlines and task dependencies.
Calendar View	Seeing upcoming due dates and milestones.
Gantt Chart View	Long-term project planning and scheduling.

To change board views:

1. Click **"Views"** in the top-right corner.
2. Select **the view that best suits your project**.

💡 **Tip: Use Kanban View** for Agile project management and **Gantt View** for strategic planning.

Final Thoughts

Your **project board is now fully set up** and ready for action! With a **clear structure, assigned tasks, and status tracking**, your team can **collaborate effectively and stay on top of deadlines**.

⬛ **You've learned how to:**

- Create and customize a project board.
- Organize tasks using groups and columns.
- Assign tasks and define progress statuses.
- Optimize project tracking with different board views.

Now that your board is set up, the next chapter will cover **Task Creation and Assignment Best Practices**, ensuring your team works efficiently and meets deadlines effectively.

Task Creation and Assignment Best Practices

Effective task management is at the heart of **successful project execution**. A poorly structured task can lead to confusion, missed deadlines, and reduced team efficiency. By following **task creation and assignment best practices** in Monday.com, project managers can ensure:

■ Clear task definitions that eliminate ambiguity.
■ Proper task assignments to the right team members.
■ Efficient prioritization and deadline management.
■ Better accountability and tracking of progress.

This chapter will guide you through the best methods to **create, assign, and manage tasks** in Monday.com to maximize productivity and ensure project success.

Step 1: Creating Clear and Actionable Tasks

A **well-defined task** should have:

1. **A Clear Name** – The task title should be descriptive yet concise.
2. **A Defined Outcome** – What needs to be achieved?
3. **A Responsible Owner** – Who is accountable for the task?
4. **A Deadline** – When is the task due?
5. **Priority Level** – How urgent is the task?

1. Naming Tasks for Clarity

Instead of vague task names like:
✗ "Write article"

Use a more specific, action-oriented title:
■ "Draft and submit Q2 marketing blog post"

💡 **Tip:** Use verbs in task names to clearly indicate actions (e.g., "Design Homepage," "Review Product Prototype").

Step 2: Assigning Tasks to the Right Team Members

Proper task assignment ensures **accountability and efficiency**. Monday.com's **People Column** allows you to assign tasks to individuals or teams.

1. How to Assign a Task in Monday.com

1. Click on the **People Column** of a task.
2. Select the **team member(s)** responsible for the task.
3. Use **@mentions** in task comments to provide additional context.

💡 **Tip:** Avoid assigning the same task to multiple people unless it requires **collaborative ownership**. If multiple team members are involved, create **subtasks** for better tracking.

Step 3: Setting Priorities for Effective Workflow

Prioritizing tasks helps teams focus on **what matters most**. Monday.com allows you to set priorities using the **Priority Column**.

Priority Level	Best For
● High Priority	Urgent, time-sensitive tasks that require immediate attention.
● Medium Priority	Important tasks with flexible deadlines.
● Low Priority	Non-urgent tasks that can be worked on when time allows.

💡 **Tip:** If your project includes **strict deadlines**, use the **Deadline Mode** to ensure that high-priority tasks are completed on time.

Step 4: Using Task Dependencies for Workflow Efficiency

Some tasks **cannot begin until another is completed**. Monday.com allows you to set **task dependencies**, ensuring **workflows move in the right sequence**.

1. How to Set Dependencies in Monday.com

1. Open the **Gantt Chart View** of your board.
2. Click on a task and select **Dependencies**.
3. Connect the task to its preceding task.

💡 **Example:**

- **Task 1:** "Design homepage wireframe" → Must be completed before
- **Task 2:** "Develop homepage UI"

💡 **Tip:** Use **automations** to trigger actions when dependent tasks are completed.

Step 5: Setting Due Dates and Reminders

Tasks without deadlines often fall behind schedule. **Always assign due dates** to keep projects moving forward.

1. Adding Due Dates to Tasks

1. Click on the **Date Column** of a task.
2. Select the due date from the calendar.
3. Use **Timeline View** for long-term scheduling.

2. Setting Task Reminders

- Use the **Automations feature** to notify assignees when tasks are approaching deadlines.
- Example: **"Send a reminder 3 days before a task is due."**

💡 **Tip:** Encourage team members to **update task statuses** regularly to avoid last-minute deadline issues.

Step 6: Breaking Down Complex Tasks with Subtasks

Large tasks can feel overwhelming. Break them down into **smaller, actionable steps** using **Subitems (Subtasks)** in Monday.com.

1. How to Add Subtasks in Monday.com

1. Click on a task.
2. Select **"Add Subitems"** under the task name.
3. Define the subtask, assign an owner, and set a deadline.

💡 **Example of a Well-Structured Task with Subtasks:**
⬛ **Task:** "Launch Email Marketing Campaign"

- **Subtask 1:** Write email content (Assigned to Content Team, Due: March 5)
- **Subtask 2:** Design email template (Assigned to Design Team, Due: March 7)
- **Subtask 3:** Schedule email send (Assigned to Marketing Lead, Due: March 10)

💡 **Tip:** Use **automation rules** to mark a task as "Completed" once all its subtasks are done.

Step 7: Automating Task Creation for Repetitive Workflows

If your team works with **recurring tasks**, use **automations** to reduce manual work.

1. Setting Up Task Automations

1. Click **"Automate"** in the board menu.
2. Choose a rule, such as:
    - **"Every Monday, create a new 'Weekly Report' task."**
    - **"When a task is marked 'Completed,' move it to 'Done'."**
3. Click **Save** to activate the automation.

💡 **Tip:** Automate **task handoffs** by setting triggers (e.g., "When Task A is completed, assign Task B to the next team member").

Step 8: Tracking Task Progress with Status Updates

A well-maintained **Status Column** helps teams track task completion **in real-time**.

Status	Meaning
🔴 In Progress	Task is currently being worked on.
🔴 Completed	Task is finished.
🔴 Stuck	Task has an issue preventing progress.
🔴 Pending Approval	Task is awaiting feedback before completion.

💡 **Tip:** Use the **Dashboard View** to monitor task statuses across multiple projects.

Best Practices for Task Management in Monday.com

■ **Keep Task Titles Clear** – Use descriptive names that specify the action.
■ **Assign the Right People** – Avoid assigning too many team members to a single task.
■ **Use Priorities Wisely** – Don't overuse "High Priority"; keep it for truly urgent tasks.
■ **Break Down Large Tasks** – Use subtasks for better tracking.
■ **Set Realistic Deadlines** – Balance due dates with team workload.
■ **Regularly Update Statuses** – Ensure tasks reflect their current progress.
■ **Automate Recurring Tasks** – Reduce manual work with automation.

Final Thoughts

Mastering **task creation and assignment best practices** in Monday.com **ensures smooth project execution**. With clear task definitions, strategic assignments, and automated workflows, you'll improve efficiency and accountability across your team.

■ **You've learned how to:**

- Create clear and structured tasks.
- Assign tasks effectively to the right team members.
- Set priorities, due dates, and dependencies.
- Use subtasks to break down complex work.
- Automate task creation for efficiency.

Now that you have a strong foundation in **task creation and assignment**, the next chapter will cover **Managing Deadlines and Dependencies**, ensuring tasks stay on track and projects move forward without delays.

Managing Deadlines and Dependencies

A project's success depends on **meeting deadlines and ensuring tasks are completed in the right order**. Managing deadlines effectively prevents delays, and properly structuring task dependencies ensures smooth workflow execution.

Monday.com offers powerful features to help **set deadlines, manage dependencies, and automate task handoffs**, keeping projects on track without confusion.

In this chapter, you'll learn how to:
- ■ **Set and track deadlines using Monday.com's Date and Timeline Columns.**
- ■ **Create and manage task dependencies to optimize workflow.**
- ■ **Use automation to prevent deadline bottlenecks.**
- ■ **Monitor upcoming deadlines using Calendar, Timeline, and Gantt Views.**

By the end, you'll have a **solid system for keeping projects on time and ensuring dependent tasks are executed smoothly**.

Step 1: Setting and Tracking Deadlines

Every task should have a clear deadline to avoid last-minute scrambles and project delays. Monday.com provides **multiple ways** to set and manage due dates.

1. Using the Date Column to Set Deadlines

The **Date Column** is the simplest way to assign deadlines to tasks.

■ **How to Add a Deadline Column:**

1. Click **"+ Add Column"** on your board.
2. Select **"Date"** and name it **"Due Date"**.
3. Click on each task and assign a deadline.

💡 **Tip:** Enable the **Deadline Mode** (found in column settings) to highlight overdue tasks automatically.

---

2. Using the Timeline Column for Scheduling

For tasks that **span multiple days or weeks**, use the **Timeline Column** to visualize project schedules.

■ **How to Add a Timeline Column:**

1. Click **"+ Add Column"** and select **"Timeline"**.
2. Click on a task and set **start and end dates**.
3. Drag the timeline bar to adjust the schedule as needed.

💡 **Tip:** The **Timeline View** (covered later) allows you to see all deadlines in a **Gantt-style layout**.

Step 2: Managing Task Dependencies

Some tasks **must be completed before others can start**. Managing **dependencies** ensures workflows move in the correct order and prevents bottlenecks.

1. Understanding Dependencies in Project Management

There are three main types of task dependencies:

Dependency Type	Example
Finish-to-Start (FS)	Task A must finish before Task B starts (e.g., "Write Blog Post" → "Publish Blog Post").
Start-to-Start (SS)	Task A and Task B must start together (e.g., "Design Website UI" & "Develop Frontend Code").
Finish-to-Finish (FF)	Task A and Task B must finish together (e.g., "Final Testing" & "Product Launch").

💡 **Tip:** The **most common dependency is Finish-to-Start**, ensuring sequential task execution.

---

2. Setting Up Dependencies in Monday.com

The **Dependency Column** helps link related tasks and ensure proper order.

🔲 **How to Add a Dependency Column:**

1. Click **"+ Add Column"** and select **"Dependency"**.
2. Choose the **task that must be completed first**.
3. Monday.com will now **prevent dependent tasks from starting too early**.

💡 **Example:**

- **Task 1:** "Write Article" → Due: March 5
- **Task 2 (Dependent on Task 1):** "Review & Edit Article" → Due: March 7

Step 3: Visualizing Deadlines and Dependencies

To avoid **missed deadlines and bottlenecks**, project managers need **real-time deadline tracking**. Monday.com provides **three key views** for better visualization.

1. Using the Calendar View

The **Calendar View** helps teams track **daily, weekly, and monthly** deadlines.

🔲 **How to Add a Calendar View:**

1. Click **"Views"** in the top-right corner of your board.
2. Select **"Calendar"** and add it to your board.
3. Filter tasks by **due date, assignee, or project phase**.

💡 **Tip:** Use **color coding** for different task categories (e.g., Marketing tasks in blue, IT tasks in green).

---

2. Using the Timeline View for Scheduling

The **Timeline View** provides a **Gantt-like** visualization, showing tasks across weeks or months.

■ **How to Add a Timeline View:**

1. Click **"Views"** and select **"Timeline"**.
2. Adjust task durations using drag-and-drop functionality.
3. Filter by **assignee, priority, or status**.

💡 **Tip:** If a task is **falling behind schedule**, adjust the timeline and notify the team automatically.

---

3. Using the Gantt Chart View for Dependencies

Gantt Charts provide **the most detailed view** of deadlines and dependencies.

■ **How to Add a Gantt Chart View:**

1. Click **"Views"** and select **"Gantt"**.
2. Link tasks using **dependencies** (dragging lines between tasks).
3. Identify the **Critical Path**—the sequence of tasks that determine project completion time.

💡 **Tip:** Tasks on the **Critical Path** cannot be delayed without delaying the entire project.

Step 4: Automating Deadline and Dependency Management

To **eliminate manual tracking**, use **Monday.com Automations** to manage deadlines and dependencies efficiently.

1. Setting Deadline Alerts

Automatically remind team members of **upcoming or overdue tasks**.

■ **How to Set a Deadline Alert:**

1. Click **"Automate"** in the board menu.
2. Select: **"When a due date arrives, notify assignee."**
3. Save the automation.

💡 **Example Automation:**

- **"If a task is overdue, change its status to 'Delayed' and notify the team."**

---

2. Automating Dependent Task Start Dates

Ensure dependent tasks **only start when prerequisites are complete**.

■ **How to Automate Dependencies:**

1. Click **"Automate"** and select:
   - **"When Task A is marked as 'Done,' move Task B to 'In Progress'."**
2. Save the rule.

💡 **Example:**

- **"When 'Draft Social Media Posts' is completed, automatically start 'Schedule Posts.'"**

Best Practices for Deadline & Dependency Management

To maximize efficiency, follow these best practices:

- **Set realistic deadlines** – Avoid overly aggressive timelines that lead to burnout.
- **Monitor progress weekly** – Use dashboards to keep track of deadlines.
- **Use dependencies wisely** – Only link tasks when necessary to avoid unnecessary restrictions.
- **Automate deadline reminders** – Reduce manual follow-ups with automation.
- **Use visual tracking** – Leverage Calendar, Timeline, and Gantt Views.

Final Thoughts

Mastering **deadline and dependency management** ensures **smooth workflow execution, prevents project delays, and keeps teams accountable**. With **clear deadlines, structured dependencies, and automation**, you can create an **efficient project management system** using Monday.com.

- **You've learned how to:**

  - Set and track deadlines using Date and Timeline Columns.
  - Manage dependencies to structure task execution.
  - Visualize deadlines with Calendar, Timeline, and Gantt Views.
  - Automate deadline reminders and task dependencies.

Now that you've established **deadline and dependency tracking**, the next chapter will cover **Tracking Progress with Status Columns**, helping teams measure project completion in real time.

Tracking Progress with Status Columns

One of the most **critical aspects of project management** is **tracking progress** efficiently. Without a clear way to monitor what's happening, tasks can get lost, deadlines may be missed, and teams can become disorganized.

Monday.com's **Status Column** provides a **visual, real-time way** to track task progress, helping teams stay aligned and making it easy to identify bottlenecks before they impact the project.

In this chapter, you'll learn how to:
■ **Set up and customize status columns for different workflows.**
■ **Use color-coded status indicators for quick updates.**
■ **Implement automation to streamline progress tracking.**
■ **Use dashboards and reporting tools to analyze project health.**

By the end, you'll have a **structured method for tracking project progress effectively** using status columns in Monday.com.

Step 1: Setting Up Status Columns

The **Status Column** in Monday.com allows you to define **custom progress indicators** that fit your workflow.

1. How to Add a Status Column

1. Open your **project board** in Monday.com.
2. Click **"+ Add Column"** at the top.
3. Select **"Status"** from the column options.
4. Click the new column header to rename it (e.g., **"Task Progress" or "Project Stage"**).

Step 2: Customizing Status Labels

A **well-structured status column** should reflect your team's workflow. Instead of using generic labels, customize them to match **your project needs**.

1. Standard Status Labels for Project Tracking

Status Label	Meaning
● To Do	The task has not started yet.
● In Progress	The task is actively being worked on.
● Completed	The task is fully completed.
● Blocked	There is an issue preventing progress.
● Pending Review	The task needs approval before completion.

💡 **Tip: Use custom colors** to make your board visually intuitive (e.g., Red for urgent blockers, Green for completed tasks).

Step 3: Creating Multiple Status Columns

Some projects require **multiple status columns** to track different aspects of progress.

Examples of Additional Status Columns

■ **"Approval Status"** → Tracks client or manager approval.
■ **"Bug Resolution Status"** → Useful for development teams tracking issue fixes.
■ **"Content Production Status"** → For marketing teams managing content creation.

To add an extra status column:

1. Click **"+ Add Column"** and select **"Status"**.
2. Name the column based on the **specific process you're tracking**.

💡 **Tip:** Use **different color schemes** for each status column to avoid confusion.

Step 4: Automating Status Updates

To **reduce manual work** and improve efficiency, **automate status changes** based on task progress.

1. How to Automate Status Updates in Monday.com

1. Click **"Automate"** in the board menu.
2. Select **"When [condition] is met, change status to [value]."**
3. Example automation rules:
   ■ **"When a due date arrives, change status to 'Overdue.'"**
   ■ **"When a task is moved to the 'Completed' group, update status to 'Done.'"**
   ■ **"When a document is uploaded, change status to 'Ready for Review.'"**

💡 **Tip:** Automating status updates **eliminates manual tracking errors** and keeps projects on track.

Step 5: Using Dashboards to Monitor Task Progress

While **Status Columns help track individual tasks**, Dashboards provide **an overview of all project progress**.

1. Key Dashboard Widgets for Status Tracking

■ **Battery Widget** – Shows overall project completion percentage.
■ **Chart Widget** – Visualizes tasks by status (e.g., Pie Chart of "In Progress" vs. "Completed" tasks).
■ **Table Widget** – Displays real-time project data across multiple boards.
■ **Workload Widget** – Ensures task distribution is balanced across team members.

2. How to Set Up a Progress Dashboard

1. Click **"Add Dashboard"** in Monday.com.
2. Select **the boards you want to track**.
3. Add widgets to monitor **task status distribution, completion rates, and blockers**.

💡 **Tip:** Use **filters to customize dashboards** by team member, task priority, or deadline range.

Step 6: Best Practices for Tracking Progress Effectively

To maximize the benefits of Status Columns, follow these best practices:

■ **Keep Status Labels Simple** – Avoid overcomplicating with too many statuses.
■ **Use Clear Colors** – Make sure status colors are intuitive (e.g., Green = Done, Red = Blocked).
■ **Automate Whenever Possible** – Reduce manual updates to improve efficiency.
■ **Regularly Review Dashboard Reports** – Identify trends in project completion rates.
■ **Encourage Team Updates** – Ensure team members regularly update task statuses.

💡 **Tip:** Conduct **weekly review meetings** using Monday.com Dashboards to analyze project health and address blockers.

Final Thoughts

Using **Status Columns effectively** ensures that your team stays aligned, deadlines are met, and projects **progress smoothly**. By customizing status labels, automating updates, and monitoring dashboards, project managers can gain **real-time insights into project health**.

■ **You've learned how to:**

- Set up and customize Status Columns.
- Automate status updates for efficiency.
- Use dashboards to track task completion.
- Implement best practices for effective progress tracking.

Now that you're tracking task progress, the next chapter will explore **Automating Repetitive Workflows**, helping you **save time and streamline project management**.

Automating Repetitive Workflows

In project management, **time is a valuable asset**. Repeating the same manual tasks—such as updating statuses, assigning tasks, and sending reminders—can slow down your workflow and increase the chances of human error.

Monday.com's **automation features** allow project managers to **eliminate repetitive work**, ensuring that processes run smoothly and consistently.

In this chapter, you'll learn how to:
- **Set up automation rules to streamline workflows.**
- **Use pre-built automation templates for common tasks.**
- **Customize automation for task assignment, deadlines, and approvals.**
- **Integrate automation with external tools for enhanced productivity.**

By the end, you'll have a **fully automated project workflow**, reducing manual effort and increasing efficiency.

Step 1: Understanding Automation in Monday.com

Automation in Monday.com works on an "If This, Then That" (IFTTT) basis, meaning that **when a trigger occurs, an action is executed automatically.**

1. The Core Components of Automation

Automation in Monday.com follows this structure:
- **Trigger** – What starts the automation (e.g., a status change, a new item added).
- **Condition (Optional)** – Any additional filters (e.g., specific assignees, priority levels).
- **Action** – What happens when the trigger is met (e.g., send a notification, move an item, update a column).

💡 **Example:**

- **Trigger:** When a task's status changes to "Done"
- **Action:** Move the task to the "Completed" group

Step 2: Setting Up Automations in Monday.com

1. How to Add an Automation Rule

1. Open your **Monday.com board**.
2. Click **"Automate"** in the top menu.
3. Select **"+ Create Custom Automation"** or choose from **pre-built automation templates**.
4. Define the **Trigger** and **Action(s)**.
5. Click **"Activate Automation"** to apply it.

💡 **Tip:** Start with simple automations before creating complex multi-step workflows.

Step 3: Common Automations to Streamline Workflows

1. Automating Task Assignments

Instead of manually assigning tasks, let Monday.com **automate it for you**.

Example Automation:

- "When a new task is added, assign it to [specific team member]."
- "When a task moves to 'In Progress,' assign it to the designated owner."

Use Case: Great for **help desks, IT support, and content production teams**.

---

2. Automating Status Updates

Manually updating task statuses can be **time-consuming**. Let automation handle it!

Example Automation:

- "When a due date arrives and the task is not marked 'Completed,' change status to 'Overdue'."
- "When a subtask is completed, update the main task status."

Use Case: Helps teams **track task completion without micromanagement**.

---

3. Automating Deadline Reminders

Never miss a deadline again by **automatically sending reminders**.

Example Automation:

- "When a task is due in 2 days, notify the assignee."
- "If a task is overdue, alert the project manager."

Use Case: Useful for **time-sensitive projects, event planning, and sprint cycles**.

---

4. Automating Recurring Tasks

Some tasks **repeat regularly** (e.g., weekly reports, monthly audits). Automate them!

Example Automation:

- "Every Monday at 9 AM, create a new 'Weekly Team Meeting' task."
- "On the 1st of every month, create a 'Prepare Monthly Report' task."

Use Case: Essential for **HR teams, finance departments, and content calendars**.

---

5. Automating Dependencies

Ensure that **dependent tasks start automatically** when prerequisites are completed.

Example Automation:

- "When Task A is completed, change Task B's status to 'In Progress'."
- "When Task A is done, notify Task B's assignee."

Use Case: Ideal for **product development, software releases, and construction projects**.

Step 4: Using Pre-Built Automation Templates

Monday.com offers **pre-made automation templates** that can be **quickly implemented**.

To access them:

1. Click **"Automate"** > **"Explore Automations"**.
2. Select from categories like:
   - **Task Management** – Auto-assign tasks, update statuses.
   - **Deadline Management** – Reminders, overdue alerts.
   - **Project Planning** – Auto-create recurring tasks.
   - **Collaboration** – Notify stakeholders, trigger approvals.

💡 **Tip: Use automation templates as a starting point** before customizing workflows to fit your needs.

Step 5: Enhancing Automations with Integrations

Monday.com **connects with other tools** to **extend automation capabilities**.

1. Popular Integrations for Automation

- **Slack** – Send task updates directly to Slack channels.
- **Google Calendar** – Sync task deadlines with your calendar.
- **Zapier** – Connect Monday.com with thousands of apps.
- **Email** – Auto-send reminders and approvals via email.

💡 **Example Automation with Slack:**

- **"When a task's status changes to 'Ready for Review,' send a message to the Slack #review-team channel."**

Step 6: Best Practices for Automating Workflows

To **maximize efficiency**, follow these best practices:

- **Start Simple** – Automate basic tasks first before adding complex logic.
- **Test Automations** – Run test cases to ensure automations work as expected.
- **Monitor Automation Logs** – Check logs to troubleshoot any failed actions.
- **Use Conditional Rules** – Apply filters to prevent unwanted automation triggers.
- **Optimize Over Time** – Review and refine automations as workflows evolve.

💡 **Tip:** Set up a **"Test Board"** before deploying automation across active projects.

Final Thoughts

Automating repetitive workflows **saves time, improves efficiency, and reduces human error**. With Monday.com's powerful automation tools, project managers can **streamline tasks, track progress effortlessly, and ensure smooth collaboration**.

■ **You've learned how to:**

- Set up automation rules.
- Use pre-built templates for common workflows.
- Automate task assignments, deadlines, and approvals.
- Integrate automation with external tools.

Now that your workflows are automated, the next chapter will explore **Using Templates for Rapid Project Setup**, helping you **standardize project workflows** and **boost productivity**.

Using Templates for Rapid Project Setup

Setting up a project from scratch can be **time-consuming and repetitive**, especially if you manage **similar types of projects regularly**. Monday.com's **templates feature** allows you to **quickly create structured project boards** with predefined columns, groups, statuses, and automations, ensuring consistency across projects.

With templates, you can:
- ■ **Save time by reusing project structures.**
- ■ **Maintain consistency across different teams and projects.**
- ■ **Ensure best practices are followed from the start.**
- ■ **Customize and refine templates to match evolving needs.**

In this chapter, you'll learn how to:

- Use **Monday.com's built-in templates**.
- Create **custom templates** for your team.
- Set up **automation and integrations** within templates.
- Optimize template usage for **scaling workflows efficiently**.

By the end of this chapter, you'll have a **fully functional project template system**, allowing you to launch new projects with minimal effort.

Step 1: Using Monday.com's Pre-Built Templates

Monday.com provides **a variety of pre-made templates** for common project types, such as:

- **Project Management** – General project tracking.
- **Marketing Planning** – Campaign and content tracking.
- **Software Development** – Agile and sprint planning.
- **HR & Recruiting** – Employee onboarding and hiring workflows.
- **Sales & CRM** – Sales pipeline and customer management.

1. How to Use a Pre-Built Template

1. **Navigate to Your Workspace** and click **"+ Add"**.
2. Select **"Choose from Templates"** from the dropdown.
3. Browse through **categories** (Project Management, Marketing, IT, etc.).
4. Click on a template to preview it.
5. Select **"Use Template"** to add it to your workspace.
6. Customize it by modifying **groups, columns, and statuses** as needed.

💡 **Tip:** Pre-built templates provide a **great starting point** but should be tailored to fit your team's specific needs.

Step 2: Creating Your Own Custom Templates

If your team follows a **specific process** that isn't covered by Monday.com's built-in templates, you can create a **custom template**.

1. How to Create a Custom Template

1. **Set Up a Board** – Create a new board and structure it according to your project needs.
2. **Customize Columns** – Add relevant columns, such as **Status, Deadline, Owner, Priority, and Notes**.
3. **Add Task Groups** – Organize tasks into groups like **"To Do," "In Progress," "Completed,"** or **project phases**.
4. **Pre-Fill Essential Items** – If certain tasks repeat in every project, add them in advance (e.g., "Kickoff Meeting," "Project Plan Approval").
5. **Set Automations** – Automate repetitive actions (e.g., auto-assign tasks, send deadline reminders).
6. **Save as a Template** – Once finalized:
   - Click **"Board Settings"** in the top-right corner.
   - Select **"Save as a Template"**.
   - Name the template and add a brief description.

💡 Tip: **Save frequently used workflows** as templates to **avoid rebuilding them each time**.

Step 3: Setting Up Automations and Integrations in Templates

To **enhance your templates**, you can **pre-configure automations and integrations** before saving them.

1. Adding Automations to Templates

Automation ensures that your workflow **runs smoothly without manual intervention**.

🔲 **Example Automations for a Project Template:**

- **"When a new task is added, assign it to [Project Manager]."**
- **"When a task moves to 'In Progress,' notify the team."**
- **"If a task is overdue, send an email reminder to the assignee."**

💡 **How to Add Automation to a Template:**

1. Click **"Automate"** on the board.
2. Choose from **pre-built automation rules** or create a custom rule.
3. Save the automation before saving the board as a template.

---

2. Connecting Integrations for Templates

If your projects **require external tools**, you can **integrate them into your template**.

🔲 **Popular Integrations for Templates:**

- **Slack** – Send task updates to team channels.
- **Google Drive** – Attach relevant documents automatically.
- **Zoom** – Schedule meetings when a task moves to "In Progress."
- **Outlook/Gmail** – Auto-send task notifications.

💡 Tip: Set up integrations **before saving your board as a template** so they apply every time the template is used.

Step 4: Optimizing Templates for Efficiency

To ensure that your templates **remain relevant and effective**, follow these optimization strategies:

■ **Keep Templates Updated** – Regularly **review and refine templates** based on team feedback.
■ **Avoid Over-Complication** – Keep templates **simple and flexible** for easy adaptation.
■ **Standardize Naming Conventions** – Use consistent **task names, columns, and statuses** across all templates.
■ **Document Template Usage** – Provide a **brief guide or checklist** explaining how to use the template effectively.
■ **Use Permissions** – Restrict template edits to **admins or project leads** to maintain consistency.

💡 **Tip:** If a template is **not working efficiently**, make adjustments and **save a new version** instead of starting from scratch.

Step 5: Scaling Project Workflows with Templates

If you manage **multiple projects** or oversee a **large team**, templates can **standardize and streamline workflows**.

1. Duplicating Templates for Multiple Projects

Instead of creating a new board **every time you start a project**, simply **duplicate an existing template**.

■ **How to Duplicate a Template for a New Project:**

1. Click **"More Actions"** (three dots) on your saved template.
2. Select **"Duplicate Board"**.
3. Choose **"Duplicate Structure Only"** (to copy settings without previous tasks) or **"Duplicate Everything"** (to include all tasks).

💡 **Use Case:** If your team runs **monthly marketing campaigns**, create a **"Marketing Campaign Template"** and duplicate it for each new campaign.

Best Practices for Using Templates

To maximize efficiency, follow these **best practices** when working with templates:

■ **Use Pre-Made Templates for Quick Setup** – Great for standard workflows.
■ **Customize Templates to Fit Your Team's Needs** – Add relevant columns, automations, and integrations.
■ **Save Frequently Used Workflows as Templates** – Avoid repetitive setup work.
■ **Keep Templates Up-to-Date** – Review and refine them periodically.
■ **Train Your Team on Template Usage** – Ensure all members understand how to apply templates effectively.

💡 **Tip: Create department-specific templates** (e.g., "Sales Pipeline Template," "HR Onboarding Template") to maintain standardization across teams.

Final Thoughts

Using **templates for rapid project setup** ensures **efficiency, consistency, and scalability** in project management. Whether using **Monday.com's built-in templates or custom ones tailored to your team's needs**, templates help you launch projects **faster and with fewer errors**.

■ **You've learned how to:**

- Use Monday.com's pre-built templates.
- Create and save custom templates for your team.
- Automate workflows and integrate tools within templates.
- Optimize and scale template usage for improved efficiency.

Now that you've **streamlined project setup with templates**, the next chapter will explore **Inviting and Managing Team Members**, ensuring **seamless collaboration and role management in Monday.com**.

Section 5:
Collaboration and Team Dynamics

Inviting and Managing Team Members

Successful project management depends on **effective collaboration**, and that starts with properly **inviting and managing team members** in Monday.com. Whether you're working with **in-house employees, freelancers, or external clients**, Monday.com allows you to **grant access, define roles, and ensure smooth communication** across teams.

By mastering team management in Monday.com, you can:
- **Ensure the right people have access to the right boards.**
- **Assign roles and permissions to control data visibility.**
- **Streamline onboarding for new team members.**
- **Use automation to simplify team collaboration.**

This chapter will cover **how to invite and manage team members**, define **permissions**, and optimize **team collaboration** in Monday.com.

Step 1: Adding Team Members to Your Monday.com Workspace

Before a team can collaborate in Monday.com, they need to be **invited to the workspace**.

1. How to Invite Team Members

1. **Go to Your Monday.com Account.**
2. Click the **Profile Icon** (top-right corner) and select **"Admin"** or **"Invite Members"**.
3. Enter the **email addresses** of the people you want to invite.
4. Select whether they should be:
   - **Members** (Full access to boards and projects).
   - **Viewers** (Read-only access).
   - **Guests** (External users with limited access).
5. Click **"Send Invite"**.

💡 **Tip:** You can invite multiple users at once by separating emails with commas.

Step 2: Understanding User Roles and Permissions

Not all team members need **full access** to every board or workspace. Monday.com provides **different permission levels** to control access.

1. Types of User Roles

Role Type	Access Level	Best For
Admin	Full access to manage team members, settings, and billing.	Project managers, Team leads.

Member	Can create and edit boards, add items, and collaborate freely.	Team members actively working on projects.
Viewer	Can only view boards and comment but not make changes.	Stakeholders, Executives, Clients needing visibility.
Guest	Limited access to specific shared boards only.	Freelancers, External partners.

💡 **Tip:** Use **Viewers** for clients who need oversight but **shouldn't edit tasks**.

Step 3: Assigning Team Members to Specific Boards

Once team members have been added to your Monday.com workspace, the next step is **granting access to relevant project boards**.

1. How to Add Team Members to a Board

1. Open the project board you want to share.
2. Click the **"Share" or "Invite"** button (top-right).
3. Select the **team members** who should have access.
4. Define whether they should be **Editors, Viewers, or Admins**.

💡 **Tip:** For sensitive projects, use **Private Boards** so only **invited team members can access them**.

Step 4: Managing Permissions and Access Control

Project managers need to **control access to specific boards, tasks, and data** to prevent unauthorized changes.

1. Board-Level Permissions

■ **Who Can Edit?** – Restrict editing rights to **specific users**.
■ **Who Can View?** – Set certain boards to **"View Only"** for stakeholders.
■ **Who Can Create Automations?** – Limit automation creation to **Admins only**.

2. Column-Level Permissions

Some columns (e.g., **Budget, Client Notes, Confidential Data**) may need **restricted access**.

■ **How to Restrict Column Access:**

1. Click on the **Column Settings** menu.
2. Select **"Restrict Column Editing"**.
3. Choose who **can and cannot edit the column**.

💡 **Use Case:** Only **Finance Team Members** should be able to **edit the budget column** while others can only view it.

Step 5: Organizing Team Members into Groups

For large teams, managing individual access can be difficult. Instead of adding people one by one, create **Team Groups** in Monday.com.

1. How to Create a Team Group

1. Go to **"Teams"** in your Monday.com workspace.
2. Click **"+ Create Team"**.
3. Name the team (e.g., **Marketing Team, Development Team, HR Team**).
4. Add relevant team members.
5. Assign the **team** to specific boards instead of adding individuals manually.

💡 **Tip:** Assigning a **team to a task** instead of individuals makes it easy to reassign tasks without reconfiguring the board.

Step 6: Automating Team Management Tasks

Instead of **manually assigning tasks and notifications**, use **Monday.com Automations** to streamline team collaboration.

🔲 **Example Automations for Team Management:**

- **"When a new task is added, auto-assign it to [specific team]."**
- **"When a task status changes to 'In Progress,' notify the assigned team member."**
- **"When a new board is created, invite the 'Marketing Team' automatically."**

💡 **Tip:** Automating assignments ensures **no task is left unassigned or forgotten**.

Step 7: Best Practices for Managing Teams Efficiently

🔲 **Use Permissions to Control Access** – Keep sensitive information secure by setting user roles.
🔲 **Group Members into Teams** – Assigning entire teams instead of individuals **simplifies access management**.
🔲 **Automate Assignments** – Reduce manual effort by **auto-assigning tasks** based on board rules.
🔲 **Regularly Review Team Access** – Remove users who no longer need access to ensure **workspace security**.
🔲 **Encourage Team Collaboration** – Use features like **@mentions and comments** to improve communication.

💡 **Tip:** Schedule **quarterly reviews** of team permissions to **prevent outdated access rights**.

Final Thoughts

Effective team management in Monday.com ensures **smooth collaboration, clear role assignments, and secure access control**. By properly **inviting, assigning, and managing team members**, project managers can **create a structured, productive work environment**.

🔲 **You've learned how to:**

- Invite and assign team members.
- Define user roles and permissions.
- Restrict access to boards and columns.
- Use automations to streamline team collaboration.

- Organize users into **Teams** for better workflow efficiency.

Now that you've set up **team collaboration**, the next chapter will cover **Real-Time Collaboration Tools: Comments and Updates**, ensuring **your team communicates efficiently within Monday.com**.

Real-Time Collaboration Tools: Comments and Updates

Effective communication is **crucial for project success**. Without a clear and structured way to share updates, ask questions, and provide feedback, teams can become **disorganized and inefficient**. Monday.com's **real-time collaboration tools**, such as **comments and updates**, ensure that **all team members stay aligned, informed, and engaged** throughout the project lifecycle.

By leveraging **real-time comments and updates**, project managers and teams can:
■ **Communicate instantly within tasks and projects.**
■ **Tag team members to ensure accountability.**
■ **Share important files, links, and discussions in one place.**
■ **Use notifications to stay updated without endless emails.**
■ **Integrate with Slack, Zoom, and email for seamless communication.**

In this chapter, you'll learn how to:

- Use **task-level comments** to centralize discussions.
- Mention and notify **team members** effectively.
- Manage **updates, files, and approvals** in one place.
- **Automate notifications** to improve workflow efficiency.

By the end, you'll have a **fully optimized collaboration system** in Monday.com, reducing email overload and increasing team productivity.

Step 1: Understanding Comments and Updates in Monday.com

Monday.com provides **built-in collaboration tools** that allow users to communicate **directly within tasks and projects** instead of relying on external messaging apps or emails.

There are **two primary collaboration features** in Monday.com:

1. **Comments** – Allow discussions at the **task level** (within a specific item).
2. **Updates** – Serve as a **running activity log** for each task, showing changes, mentions, and discussions.

💡 **Why Use These Features?**
■ No more scattered communication across email, chat, and meetings.
■ Centralized discussions within relevant tasks.
■ Team members receive real-time notifications for updates.

Step 2: Adding and Managing Comments

1. How to Add a Comment to a Task

1. Open a board and select a **task (item)**.
2. Click the **speech bubble icon** or the **"Updates"** section.
3. Type your comment.
4. Click **"Post"** to submit it.

💡 **Tip:** Use comments to **provide task updates, request feedback, or clarify project details**.

2. Using @Mentions to Notify Team Members

Monday.com allows users to **tag specific team members** within comments to ensure they see important updates.

■ **How to Mention Someone in a Comment:**

- Type "@" followed by the team member's name (e.g., **"@John Please review this by Friday."**).
- The mentioned user will receive **an instant notification**.

💡 **Use Case:** If you need approval on a report, comment:
"@Anna Can you review this and approve it by EOD?"

■ **How to Mention Entire Teams:**

- Type **"@team"** to notify the **entire project team**.
- Type **"@here"** to notify **only active online users**.

💡 **Tip:** Avoid **overusing @mentions** to prevent notification fatigue.

Step 3: Managing Updates and Task History

Every task in Monday.com has an "Updates" section, which acts as a **timeline of conversations, file attachments, and status changes**.

1. How to View Updates for a Task

1. Click on a task (item) in a board.
2. Select the **"Updates"** tab.
3. Scroll to see a **timeline of comments, mentions, and status changes**.

■ **Why Updates Matter:**

- See **who changed a task's status** and when.
- Track **conversations related to the task** in one place.
- Attach **files, images, and links** for reference.

💡 **Use Case:** Need to check **why a deadline was changed?** Just go to **Updates** and see the history.

Step 4: Sharing Files and Attachments in Comments

Instead of sending **files via email**, Monday.com allows you to **attach documents directly to task comments**.

1. How to Attach a File to a Comment

1. Open the task's **"Updates"** section.
2. Click the **paperclip icon** to upload a file.
3. Select a document from your **computer, Google Drive, or Dropbox**.
4. Click **"Post"** to share.

💡 **Use Case:** Upload a **presentation draft** in the comments for team review.

Step 5: Automating Notifications for Important Updates

Instead of **manually notifying team members**, set up **automations** to keep everyone updated.

1. Setting Up Automatic Notifications

■ **Example Automations:**

- **"When a task's status changes to 'Completed,' notify the project manager."**
- **"If a task is overdue, send a reminder to the assignee."**
- **"When a file is uploaded, notify the relevant team members."**

■ **How to Automate Notifications:**

1. Click **"Automate"** at the top of your board.
2. Select **"Notify someone when…"** as the trigger.
3. Set the condition (e.g., **when a task is assigned, when a due date is reached**).
4. Choose the user(s) to receive the notification.
5. Click **"Activate"**.

💡 Tip: Automate **weekly status reports** to be sent via email every Monday.

Step 6: Integrating External Communication Tools

If your team **uses Slack, Zoom, or email**, you can **integrate these tools** with Monday.com for better communication.

1. Slack Integration

- Automatically **send task updates** to a Slack channel.
- Example: **"When a task is assigned, send a Slack message to @team."**

2. Zoom Integration

- Link **Zoom meetings** directly to Monday.com boards.
- Example: **"Schedule a Zoom call when a task is marked 'Review Needed.'"**

3. Email Integration

- Convert **emails into Monday.com tasks automatically**.
- Example: **"Forward client emails to Monday.com to create new items."**

💡 Tip: Reduce email overload by **handling discussions directly in Monday.com**.

Step 7: Best Practices for Effective Collaboration

■ **Use @mentions wisely** – Notify **only necessary team members** to avoid spam.
■ **Attach relevant files** – Keep all **project documents within task comments**.
■ **Automate notifications** – Prevent **missed deadlines and status updates**.
■ **Integrate with Slack & Email** – Streamline **cross-platform communication**.
■ **Encourage team adoption** – Train your team to **use comments instead of emails**.

💡 Tip: Schedule a **weekly review** of all comments and updates to **ensure alignment**.

Final Thoughts

Using **real-time collaboration tools like comments and updates** helps project teams **stay aligned, reduce unnecessary emails, and centralize communication**. With @mentions, file sharing, and **automated notifications**, Monday.com ensures that your team **never misses critical information**.

You've learned how to:

- Use comments and updates for **real-time discussions**.
- Notify team members using **@mentions and automated alerts**.
- Attach **files and documents** within tasks.
- Integrate **Slack, Zoom, and email for streamlined communication**.
- Automate **task notifications to improve efficiency**.

Now that your team is communicating effectively, the next chapter will explore **File Sharing and Document Management**, helping you **organize and manage project files efficiently** in Monday.com.

File Sharing and Document Management

In any project, **efficient file sharing and document management** are essential for **collaboration, organization, and accountability**. Teams frequently exchange **reports, presentations, images, spreadsheets, and contracts**, making it crucial to store and access these files **in one central location** rather than scattered across multiple platforms.

Monday.com offers **robust file-sharing features** that allow teams to:
■ **Store and access documents directly within tasks.**
■ **Collaborate on files without switching between platforms.**
■ **Organize attachments efficiently within boards and updates.**
■ **Integrate with cloud storage tools like Google Drive, Dropbox, and OneDrive.**

This chapter will guide you through **how to manage files effectively within Monday.com**, ensuring your team has **quick and structured access to critical documents**.

Step 1: Uploading and Attaching Files in Monday.com

Monday.com allows users to **upload files directly into tasks**, ensuring that all relevant documents are stored within the project board.

1. How to Upload Files to a Task

1. Open a board and select the **task (item)** where you want to attach a file.
2. Click the **"Updates"** section.
3. Click the **paperclip icon** or drag and drop a file.
4. Select a document from your **computer, Google Drive, Dropbox, or OneDrive**.
5. Click **"Post"** to attach the file.

■ **Supported File Types:**

- **Documents** (PDF, Word, Google Docs)
- **Spreadsheets** (Excel, Google Sheets)
- **Images** (PNG, JPEG, GIF)
- **Videos** (MP4, MOV)

❗ **Tip:** Rename files before uploading them to **ensure clarity and easy retrieval**.

Step 2: Organizing Files Efficiently

As files accumulate, organizing them effectively within Monday.com **prevents clutter and confusion**.

1. Using the File Column for Centralized Storage

Instead of attaching documents in multiple updates, use the **File Column** to store **all key project documents in one place**.

■ **How to Add a File Column to a Board:**

1. Click **"+ Add Column"** at the top of the board.
2. Select **"File"** from the column options.
3. Click on a task and upload or attach a document.

💡 **Use Case:** Create a **"Project Assets" column** to store **brand guidelines, contracts, and reference materials**.

Step 3: Collaborating on Files with Comments and Updates

Teams often need to **collaborate, provide feedback, and track file revisions**. Monday.com enables **real-time discussions** on uploaded documents.

1. How to Leave Comments on Files

1. Click on the uploaded file in the **Updates** section.
2. Use the **comment box** to provide feedback or request changes.
3. Use **@mentions** (e.g., **"@John Please revise this by tomorrow."**) to notify team members.

💡 **Tip:** Keep conversations **within Monday.com** instead of using external emails to avoid miscommunication.

Step 4: Version Control and File History

To prevent **confusion over document versions**, Monday.com **tracks file updates automatically**.

1. Managing Document Versions

⬛ **When a new version of a file is uploaded**, the system retains the older version for reference.
⬛ **Team members can compare different versions** and restore previous files if needed.

💡 **Use Case:** When working on **contract negotiations**, ensure **only the latest approved version is used**.

Step 5: Integrating Monday.com with Cloud Storage Tools

If your team stores documents **in Google Drive, Dropbox, or OneDrive**, you can **integrate these tools into Monday.com** for seamless access.

1. How to Connect Google Drive, Dropbox, or OneDrive

1. Click on a **task (item)** and go to the **Updates** section.
2. Click the **cloud storage icon**.
3. Select **Google Drive, Dropbox, or OneDrive**.
4. Log into your cloud account and select the file to attach.

⬛ **Why Use Cloud Storage Integrations?**

- Eliminates **duplicate file uploads**.
- Ensures **team members access the latest version**.
- Saves **storage space in Monday.com**.

💡 **Tip:** Use **Google Docs for collaborative editing** without downloading and re-uploading files.

Step 6: Automating File Management

Manually managing file attachments **can be time-consuming**. Automating workflows **streamlines document handling**.

1. Automating File Attachments and Approvals

■ **Example Automations:**

- **"When a file is uploaded, notify the project manager for approval."**
- **"When a task moves to 'Final Review,' request file upload."**
- **"When a file is uploaded, change task status to 'Waiting for Feedback'."**

■ **How to Set Up File Automations:**

1. Click **"Automate"** in your board menu.
2. Select a **trigger** (e.g., **"When a file is added…"**).
3. Define an **action** (e.g., **"Send a notification"** or **"Change status."**).
4. Click **"Save"** to activate automation.

💡 **Tip:** Automate **file approval processes** for marketing materials, legal contracts, and design assets.

Step 7: Best Practices for Effective File Sharing

To ensure **smooth file management**, follow these best practices:

■ **Use Naming Conventions** – Keep file names **consistent and clear** (e.g., "Marketing_Plan_Q3_2024.pdf").
■ **Organize by Project Phase** – Store files in **separate columns or boards** based on **project stage**.
■ **Encourage Cloud Storage Usage** – Reduces **file duplication and version confusion**.
■ **Automate File Approvals** – Saves time and ensures **team alignment**.
■ **Regularly Archive Old Files** – Move outdated files to an **"Archive" board** to prevent clutter.

💡 **Tip:** Conduct **monthly file audits** to keep storage clean and organized.

Final Thoughts

Managing **file sharing and document storage** in Monday.com ensures **seamless collaboration, easy access, and reduced version confusion**. By using **File Columns, Cloud Integrations, and Automations**, project teams can keep **documents structured and readily available**.

■ **You've learned how to:**

- Upload and attach files to tasks.
- Organize files with **File Columns**.
- Collaborate using **comments and version control**.
- Integrate cloud storage tools.
- Automate **file approval workflows**.

Now that you've mastered file management, the next chapter will cover **Integrating Communication Tools (Slack, Zoom, etc.)**, helping your team **improve collaboration beyond Monday.com**.

Integrating Communication Tools (Slack, Zoom, etc.)

Seamless communication is the backbone of **efficient project management**. While Monday.com offers built-in collaboration tools, integrating **external communication platforms** like **Slack, Zoom, Microsoft Teams, and email** enhances **team connectivity, responsiveness, and workflow efficiency**.

By integrating these tools, teams can:
- **Reduce the need for constant email updates.**
- **Receive instant notifications for task updates.**
- **Host meetings and discussions without leaving Monday.com.**
- **Sync conversations with project progress automatically.**

This chapter will guide you through **how to integrate and use Slack, Zoom, Microsoft Teams, and email within Monday.com**, ensuring your team stays aligned and connected.

Step 1: Integrating Slack with Monday.com

Slack is one of the most widely used communication tools for teams. By integrating it with Monday.com, you can **automate updates, send task notifications, and streamline discussions**.

1. How to Connect Monday.com with Slack

1. Open **Monday.com** and go to the board you want to integrate.
2. Click **"Integrate"** (top-right menu).
3. Search for **"Slack"** and select it.
4. Click **"Add to Slack"** and follow the authorization process.
5. Choose which Slack channel to link with Monday.com.

- **Use Case:** Automatically **send notifications to a Slack channel** when a task is updated.

---

2. Automating Slack Notifications for Task Updates

After integrating Slack, you can **set up automated alerts** to keep your team informed.

- **Example Automations:**

  - **"When a task's status changes to 'In Progress,' send a Slack message to @team."**
  - **"When a deadline is missed, notify the Slack #project-updates channel."**
  - **"When a task is completed, send a 'Well done!' message in Slack."**

💡 **Tip:** Use Slack integration to **reduce unnecessary emails and keep updates centralized**.

Step 2: Using Zoom for Virtual Meetings in Monday.com

Virtual meetings are essential for **team collaboration, client discussions, and project planning**. Instead of manually scheduling and tracking meetings, **Zoom integration allows you to create, join, and track meetings directly in Monday.com**.

1. How to Integrate Zoom with Monday.com

1. Open **Monday.com** and go to **"Integrations"**.
2. Search for **"Zoom"** and click **"Add Integration"**.
3. Log in to your **Zoom account** and authorize the connection.

■ **Use Case:** Schedule Zoom meetings **automatically when a task reaches a certain status** (e.g., "Review Needed").

---

2. Automating Zoom Meeting Scheduling

Instead of **manually creating Zoom links**, automate meeting scheduling **based on project progress**.

■ **Example Automations:**

- **"When a task moves to 'Client Review,' schedule a Zoom call and send invites."**
- **"When a team meeting is scheduled in Monday.com, create a Zoom link."**

💡 **Tip:** Add a **Zoom Meeting Column** to store links for easy access.

Step 3: Integrating Microsoft Teams for Unified Communication

Microsoft Teams is a popular tool for **real-time chat, file sharing, and video conferencing**. Integrating it with Monday.com enhances team collaboration **without switching between platforms**.

1. How to Integrate Microsoft Teams

1. Open **Monday.com** and navigate to **"Integrations"**.
2. Search for **"Microsoft Teams"** and select it.
3. Click **"Add to Microsoft Teams"** and authorize access.
4. Choose a **Teams channel** for notifications and updates.

■ **Use Case:** Post **task updates, due dates, and project milestones** to a Teams channel.

---

2. Automating Notifications in Microsoft Teams

You can set up automation to **send updates directly to a Teams chat** when changes occur in Monday.com.

■ **Example Automations:**

- **"When a new task is created, send a message to the Teams project group."**
- **"When a deadline is missed, send an alert to the project manager in Teams."**

💡 **Tip:** Use **Teams chatbots** to pull project reports from Monday.com automatically.

Step 4: Connecting Monday.com to Email for Task Updates

For teams that **rely on email notifications**, integrating Monday.com with Gmail or Outlook helps **automate updates, send reminders, and track progress** without logging into Monday.com frequently.

1. How to Integrate Email with Monday.com

1. Go to **Monday.com > Integrations**.
2. Search for **Gmail** or **Outlook** and select it.
3. Click **"Connect"** and log in to your email account.
4. Choose **how email notifications should be sent** (e.g., on task updates, status changes).

■ **Use Case:** Send automatic **email notifications when tasks are assigned or updated**.

---

2. Automating Email Notifications for Project Updates

Instead of **manually updating team members via email**, set up automation to **send email reminders based on project activity**.

■ **Example Automations:**

- **"When a task is assigned, send an email notification to the assignee."**
- **"When a project deadline is 2 days away, send a reminder email to the team."**
- **"When a task status changes to 'Client Review,' notify the client via email."**

💡 **Tip:** Use email templates to **personalize task notifications** and save time.

Step 5: Best Practices for Integrating Communication Tools

To ensure **effective collaboration across multiple platforms**, follow these best practices:

■ **Limit Notifications to Essentials** – Avoid overwhelming the team with **too many alerts**.
■ **Use Slack for Quick Updates, Email for Formal Approvals** – Balance **instant messaging and email communication**.
■ **Automate Notifications for Key Milestones** – Send **alerts only for critical changes**.
■ **Centralize Meeting Links** – Store Zoom/Teams meeting links **in a dedicated column**.
■ **Regularly Review Integrations** – Ensure **tools are optimized for your team's workflow**.

💡 **Tip: Host a training session** for your team on how to use **integrated tools effectively**.

Final Thoughts

Integrating **Slack, Zoom, Microsoft Teams, and email with Monday.com** creates a **streamlined communication system** that **reduces manual updates, improves responsiveness, and enhances collaboration**.

■ **You've learned how to:**

- Connect **Slack, Zoom, and Microsoft Teams** for better communication.
- Automate **task notifications and meeting scheduling**.
- Use **email integrations** to notify stakeholders.
- Apply **best practices** to optimize tool usage.

Now that your team is communicating seamlessly, the next chapter will explore **Handling Feedback and Revisions Efficiently**, ensuring **smooth collaboration and project adjustments** in Monday.com.

Handling Feedback and Revisions Efficiently

Feedback is an essential part of **project management, task refinement, and team collaboration**. Without a structured approach, revisions can become chaotic, leading to **missed updates, duplicate work, or miscommunication**.

Monday.com provides robust tools to **streamline feedback collection, track revisions, and ensure accountability**, reducing back-and-forth emails and misaligned expectations.

By leveraging Monday.com's features for handling feedback and revisions, project managers and teams can:
- **Centralize all feedback within tasks for easy reference.**
- **Use status updates to track revisions and approvals.**
- **Tag team members for clarity and accountability.**
- **Automate reminders for pending revisions.**
- **Integrate external review tools for seamless collaboration.**

This chapter will cover **how to manage feedback efficiently within Monday.com**, ensuring that revisions are **organized, trackable, and aligned with project goals**.

Step 1: Using Comments for Task-Specific Feedback

Monday.com allows users to **leave feedback directly on tasks** using the **comments section within the Updates tab**. This ensures that all discussions are tied to **the relevant item** instead of scattered across emails or messaging apps.

1. How to Add Feedback to a Task

1. Open a **task (item)** within a board.
2. Navigate to the **"Updates"** section.
3. Click **"Add a Comment"** and type your feedback.
4. Use **@mentions** (e.g., **@John**) to tag specific team members.
5. Click **"Post"** to save the feedback.

💡 **Use Case:** Instead of sending multiple emails, team members can **comment directly on tasks**, keeping feedback **organized and visible to all stakeholders**.

Step 2: Managing Feedback with Status Updates

Using status columns to track feedback and revisions ensures **clear visibility of progress**.

1. Creating a Feedback Status Column

1. Click **"+ Add Column"** in your board.
2. Select **"Status"** and rename it to **"Feedback Status"**.
3. Define custom statuses such as:
   - **Needs Review**
   - **Pending Edits**
   - **Approved**
   - **Rejected**

💡 **Tip:** This method ensures that **everyone knows the current state of feedback and whether revisions are required**.

Step 3: Assigning Feedback Tasks

When feedback requires **specific actions**, it should be assigned as a separate task.

1. How to Create a Feedback Task

1. Open the project board.
2. Click **"+ Add Item"** and name the task **(e.g., Revise Marketing Presentation)**.
3. Assign the task to **the person responsible for revisions**.
4. Add **a due date** for the revisions.
5. Attach the relevant document and add a comment with **specific instructions**.

💡 **Use Case:** If a design draft needs changes, create a task named **"Design Revisions – Landing Page"**, assign it to the designer, and set a deadline.

Step 4: Tracking and Managing Multiple Revisions

When multiple revisions are required, tracking them manually can **lead to confusion**. Monday.com's **Version Control & File History** keeps things organized.

1. Managing Versions of a Document

■ Upload **new versions of a document** without deleting previous ones.
■ Keep a **file history** so you can revert to an older version if needed.
■ Add a **comment specifying what has changed** in each version.

💡 **How to Upload and Track Document Revisions:**

1. Click on a task and navigate to **"Updates"**.
2. Attach the revised document.
3. Add a comment describing **what was changed**.
4. Tag the reviewer **(@ProjectManager) for approval**.

💡 **Tip:** Label file versions **clearly** (e.g., **Proposal_v1.pdf, Proposal_v2.pdf**) to avoid confusion.

Step 5: Automating Feedback Reminders

Instead of manually following up on revisions, **automate notifications** to keep feedback loops moving.

1. Setting Up Automated Feedback Reminders

■ **Example Automations:**

- **"When feedback is added, notify the assigned team member."**
- **"When a task is in 'Needs Review' for more than 2 days, send a reminder."**
- **"If a revision task is overdue, notify the project manager."**

■ **How to Automate Feedback Requests:**

1. Click **"Automate"** in the board menu.

2. Select a trigger (e.g., **"When a task's status is 'Needs Review'…"**).
3. Define an action (e.g., **"Send a reminder to the assignee."**).
4. Click **"Activate"** to set the automation live.

💡 **Tip:** Use these reminders to **ensure that feedback is addressed in a timely manner** without constant manual follow-ups.

Step 6: Integrating External Review Tools

For teams using **Google Docs, Figma, Adobe Creative Cloud, or other collaboration platforms**, integrating these tools with Monday.com makes feedback management **even smoother**.

1. Connecting Monday.com to Review Tools

- **Google Docs** – Attach documents directly to Monday.com tasks.
- **Figma** – Link design files for real-time collaboration.
- **Adobe Creative Cloud** – Manage creative revisions seamlessly.

■ **How to Attach External Review Links:**

1. Open a task in **Monday.com**.
2. Click **"Attach File"** and select **"Link"**.
3. Paste the link to the external document.
4. Add a **comment describing what needs review**.

💡 **Use Case:** Instead of downloading a document and re-uploading every revision, simply **link to Google Docs or Figma** for real-time feedback.

Step 7: Best Practices for Managing Feedback in Monday.com

To optimize feedback and revision processes, follow these best practices:

■ **Centralize Feedback** – Keep all **comments and revision history in Monday.com** instead of using emails.
■ **Use Status Updates for Transparency** – Ensure everyone knows **what's pending, what's approved, and what needs revision**.
■ **Assign Clear Deadlines for Revisions** – Prevent bottlenecks by setting **specific due dates**.
■ **Automate Reminders to Reduce Delays** – Use **notifications to keep work on track**.
■ **Integrate with Review Tools** – Eliminate unnecessary downloads by linking **Google Docs, Figma, or Dropbox** directly to tasks.

💡 **Tip:** Schedule **weekly feedback review meetings** using Monday.com's Zoom or Teams integration to discuss pending revisions.

Final Thoughts

Effectively handling **feedback and revisions** in Monday.com helps teams **stay aligned, reduce confusion, and improve productivity**. By **centralizing feedback, automating reminders, and integrating review tools**, project managers can ensure that **tasks are refined efficiently without unnecessary delays**.

■ **You've learned how to:**

- Use **comments and @mentions** for feedback.
- Track **revision statuses with status columns**.
- Assign **feedback tasks with deadlines**.
- Automate **reminders to speed up reviews**.
- Integrate **external review tools for seamless collaboration**.

Now that your feedback process is streamlined, the next section will cover **Advanced Techniques for Project Success: Automations and Custom Rules**, helping you **eliminate manual tasks and optimize workflows in Monday.com**.

Section 6:
Advanced Techniques for Project Success

Automations: Saving Time with Custom Rules

Manual tasks—such as updating statuses, assigning tasks, and sending notifications—consume **valuable time** and increase the risk of **delays and errors**. **Monday.com automations** help project managers **eliminate repetitive work**, ensuring that teams stay focused on high-priority tasks.

By leveraging **custom automations**, you can:
- **Reduce manual workload by automating routine tasks.**
- **Ensure consistency in task tracking and status updates.**
- **Trigger notifications and reminders for deadlines.**
- **Optimize team collaboration with automatic task assignments.**
- **Improve efficiency by integrating with third-party tools like Slack, email, and calendars.**

This chapter will guide you through **creating and managing automations** to enhance your project workflow in Monday.com.

Step 1: Understanding Automations in Monday.com

Automations in Monday.com are **custom rules** that execute specific actions based on predefined triggers. These follow the **"When X happens, do Y"** structure.

Common Automation Examples:

- **"When a task is marked as 'In Progress,' notify the assigned team member."**
- **"When a due date is reached, send a reminder to the project owner."**
- **"When a task is completed, move it to the 'Done' group."**
- **"When a new item is created, assign it to the project lead automatically."**

💡 **Use Case:** Instead of manually checking deadlines, you can set up an automation to **remind users when a task is due in 24 hours**.

Step 2: Creating a Basic Automation

1. How to Set Up an Automation

1. Open your **Monday.com workspace** and go to a board.
2. Click **"Automate"** in the top menu.
3. Select **"Create Custom Automation."**
4. Choose a **Trigger (When X happens…)** – Example: **"When status changes to 'Done'"**.
5. Select an **Action (Do Y…)** – Example: **"Move the task to 'Completed' group"**.
6. Click **"Create Automation"** and activate it.

💡 **Tip:** Start with **basic automations**, then gradually add complexity as needed.

Step 3: Automating Task Assignments

Assigning tasks manually can be time-consuming, especially in large projects. Automate this process so that **tasks are assigned based on status, priority, or category**.

1. Automating Task Assignment Based on Status

■ Example Automation:

- **"When a new task is added, assign it to [Project Manager]."**
- **"When a task moves to 'Urgent,' assign it to the senior team member."**

💡 Use Case: If a new **marketing request** is created, you can **automatically assign it to the marketing lead**.

2. Assigning Tasks Based on Task Type

You can also create rules based on **task categories**.

■ Example Automation:

- **"When a task is tagged as 'Design,' assign it to the design team."**
- **"When a task is tagged as 'Bug Fix,' assign it to the QA team."**

💡 Tip: This ensures that tasks **always land in the right hands** without manual intervention.

Step 4: Automating Notifications and Reminders

Staying on top of deadlines is crucial for **timely project completion**. Automate reminders to **reduce delays** and keep team members informed.

1. Setting Up Deadline Reminders

■ Example Automation:

- **"When a task is due in 24 hours, notify the assignee."**
- **"When a task is overdue, send an email alert to the project manager."**

💡 Use Case: If a **client deliverable is due soon**, set an automatic reminder **48 hours before the deadline**.

2. Automating Status Updates with Notifications

■ Example Automation:

- **"When a task moves to 'Review Needed,' notify the team lead."**
- **"When a project phase is completed, notify stakeholders."**

💡 Tip: Avoid overwhelming team members with notifications—set them only for **critical updates**.

Step 5: Automating Workflows for Efficiency

Beyond simple notifications and assignments, **Monday.com allows for complex workflow automation** to optimize processes.

1. Moving Tasks Automatically Based on Progress

■ **Example Automation:**

- "When a task's status changes to 'Completed,' move it to the 'Done' group."
- "When a sales lead is marked as 'Interested,' move it to the 'Follow-up' board."

💡 **Use Case:** If a **product launch** goes live, **automatically move related tasks to the 'Completed' phase**.

2. Using Conditional Logic for Workflows

Monday.com supports **conditional logic**, allowing for **if/then workflows**.

■ **Example Automation:**

- "If a task is assigned to Marketing and is overdue, notify the marketing manager."
- "If a high-priority task is created, notify the leadership team immediately."

💡 **Tip:** Conditional logic ensures **different workflows are triggered based on task properties**.

Step 6: Integrating Automations with External Tools

Monday.com automations can **connect with third-party apps** to expand functionality.

1. Slack and Microsoft Teams Notifications

■ **Example Automation:**

- "When a project milestone is reached, send an update to the Slack #projects channel."

2. Syncing with Google Calendar or Outlook

■ **Example Automation:**

- "When a task deadline is added, sync it with the team calendar."

💡 **Use Case:** Automatically add **meeting schedules to Outlook or Google Calendar** when tasks are created.

Step 7: Best Practices for Automating Workflows

■ **Keep Automations Simple** – Start with **basic automations** before adding complexity.
■ **Test Automations Before Relying on Them** – Run **test scenarios** to ensure they work correctly.
■ **Avoid Overloading with Notifications** – Too many notifications can **reduce effectiveness**.
■ **Regularly Review Automations** – Adjust **automations based on workflow changes**.
■ **Use Conditional Logic for Efficiency** – Ensure **automations adapt to different situations**.

💡 **Tip:** Create an **"Automation Log Board"** to track all active automations and review their performance.

Final Thoughts

Automations in Monday.com eliminate manual work, streamline task management, and improve productivity. By setting up **custom rules for assignments, notifications, and workflow automation**, project managers can focus on **high-value tasks instead of repetitive work**.

■ You've learned how to:

- Create **custom automation rules** in Monday.com.
- Automate **task assignments, notifications, and workflow transitions**.
- Set up **reminders for deadlines and critical updates**.
- Use **conditional logic** for advanced workflows.
- Integrate **Slack, email, and calendar tools** for seamless communication.

Now that you've automated **routine tasks**, the next chapter will focus on **Time Tracking and Reporting for Accountability**, helping you **monitor project progress and team efficiency in Monday.com**.

Time Tracking and Reporting for Accountability

Time is one of the most valuable resources in **project management**. Without a structured way to **track time spent on tasks**, teams risk **missed deadlines, inefficiencies, and resource misallocation**. Monday.com's **time tracking and reporting tools** ensure that project managers have **real-time visibility into productivity**, helping them optimize **workloads, timelines, and overall accountability**.

By leveraging **Monday.com's time tracking and reporting features**, project managers can:
■ **Monitor how much time is spent on tasks** to improve efficiency.
■ **Identify productivity bottlenecks** and areas of improvement.
■ **Track billable hours** for client-based projects.
■ **Generate detailed reports** for management and stakeholders.
■ **Improve project estimation and planning for future tasks.**

This chapter will guide you through **setting up time tracking, creating reports, and using insights** to enhance team accountability in Monday.com.

Step 1: Enabling the Time Tracking Column

Monday.com provides a **Time Tracking Column** that allows users to **log hours directly within tasks**.

1. How to Add a Time Tracking Column

1. Open your **Monday.com board** where you manage projects.
2. Click **"+ Add Column"** at the top.
3. Search for **"Time Tracking"** and select it.
4. The column is now added, allowing users to **start/stop a timer** when working on a task.

💡 **Tip:** Ensure all team members **log their hours consistently** for accurate reporting.

Step 2: Tracking Time Spent on Tasks

Once the **Time Tracking Column** is set up, users can **log time manually or use the built-in timer**.

1. How to Start and Stop Time Tracking

1. Click on the **Time Tracking Column** for a specific task.
2. Click **"Start Timer"** when beginning work.
3. Click **"Stop Timer"** when finished.
4. The system automatically logs the time spent on the task.

■ **Alternative Method:** If a team member forgot to start the timer, they can **manually enter the hours worked**.

💡 **Use Case:** A designer working on a **marketing campaign** can start the timer when they begin designing and stop it when they finish. This ensures accurate tracking of effort.

Step 3: Generating Time Tracking Reports

Once time is logged, **Monday.com provides powerful reporting features** to analyze productivity and project efficiency.

1. How to Create a Time Tracking Report

1. Navigate to your **Monday.com board**.
2. Click on the **"Dashboard"** section.
3. Select **"Add Widget"** and search for **"Time Tracking"**.
4. Choose how you want to visualize the data (**bar chart, pie chart, timeline**).
5. Set filters such as **date range, team members, and project types**.

▓ **Types of Reports You Can Generate:**

- **Total hours spent per project**
- **Time spent per team member**
- **Average time spent on task completion**
- **Billable vs. non-billable hours**

💡 **Use Case:** A project manager can generate a **monthly report on team productivity** to analyze **which tasks consume the most time**.

Step 4: Automating Time Tracking Alerts

To prevent missed time entries, set up **automated reminders** in Monday.com.

1. Setting Up Time Tracking Reminders

▓ **Example Automations:**

- **"If a task is in progress for more than 2 hours, send a reminder to log time."**
- **"At the end of each workday, remind team members to log their hours."**

2. How to Create an Automation for Time Tracking

1. Click **"Automate"** in the board menu.
2. Select a trigger (**e.g., "At 6 PM, remind users to log their hours"**).
3. Choose an action (**e.g., "Send a notification to the team"**).
4. Click **"Save"** to activate the automation.

💡 **Tip:** Automate time tracking reminders **to ensure accurate data collection**.

Step 5: Using Time Tracking for Client Billing

For teams working on **billable projects**, Monday.com's time tracking feature **simplifies invoice generation and cost analysis**.

1. How to Track Billable Hours

▓ **Create a Custom Column for Billable vs. Non-Billable Work:**

1. Click **"+ Add Column"** → Select **Dropdown Column**.
2. Add options like **Billable, Non-Billable, Internal Work**.
3. Use filters to calculate **billable vs. non-billable hours**.

2. Exporting Time Tracking Data for Billing

1. Open the **Time Tracking Report**.

2. Click **Export → Download as CSV or Excel**.
3. Use this data to generate **invoices for clients**.

💡 **Use Case:** A **freelance agency** can **export tracked hours** and **invoice clients based on actual work completed**.

Step 6: Optimizing Workflows Based on Time Reports

Time tracking is **not just for logging hours**—it helps optimize workflows by **identifying inefficiencies**.

1. Identifying Productivity Bottlenecks

🔲 **Example Insights from Time Reports:**

- Tasks that **take longer than estimated** → Need **workflow improvement**.
- Team members **overloaded with work** → Adjust assignments for balance.
- **Repetitive tasks consuming excessive time** → Consider **automation or delegation**.

💡 **Use Case:** If developers **spend excessive time on bug fixes**, management can **invest in better debugging tools or training**.

Step 7: Best Practices for Time Tracking and Reporting

🔲 **Standardize Time Logging** – Ensure **all team members track time consistently**.
🔲 **Use Labels for Billable Work** – Separate **billable vs. non-billable hours**.
🔲 **Automate Time Tracking Reminders** – Reduce **missed time entries**.
🔲 **Analyze Time Data Weekly** – Identify **inefficiencies and improve workflows**.
🔲 **Integrate Time Tracking with Payroll** – Simplify **salary and client invoicing**.

💡 **Tip:** Hold **weekly team reviews** to discuss **time tracking reports** and **optimize workflows accordingly**.

Final Thoughts

Time tracking and reporting in Monday.com help project managers ensure accountability, **improve efficiency, and optimize resource allocation**. By implementing **structured time tracking, automated reminders, and insightful reporting**, teams can **eliminate inefficiencies and boost productivity**.

🔲 **You've learned how to:**

- Set up **time tracking columns** for accurate logging.
- Generate **reports for productivity insights**.
- Automate **reminders to ensure accurate data collection**.
- Use **time tracking for client billing**.
- Optimize **workflows based on time analysis**.

Now that you've mastered **time tracking**, the next chapter will cover **Managing Workloads with the Workload View**, helping you **balance team capacity and prevent burnout** in Monday.com.

Managing Workloads with the Workload View

Effective **workload management** is key to ensuring that tasks are distributed **fairly and efficiently** across teams. Without proper tracking, some team members may be **overloaded with tasks**, while others remain underutilized.

The **Workload View in Monday.com** allows project managers to:
■ **Visualize task distribution across team members.**
■ **Identify bottlenecks before they impact project timelines.**
■ **Balance workloads to prevent burnout.**
■ **Ensure deadlines are met without overwhelming employees.**
■ **Optimize resource allocation for better project execution.**

This chapter will guide you through **setting up and using the Workload View in Monday.com**, helping you ensure that tasks are assigned efficiently and workloads remain balanced.

Step 1: Understanding the Workload View

The **Workload View** in Monday.com provides a **visual representation of how tasks are distributed across team members**. It displays:

- **Who is working on what tasks** and when.
- **How many tasks each team member has** on their plate.
- **Whether someone is overloaded or underutilized.**

💡 **Use Case:** A project manager can **quickly see if one developer has 10 tasks while another has only 2** and **reassign work accordingly**.

Step 2: Adding the Workload View to a Board

To start managing team capacity, you need to **add the Workload View** to your project board.

1. How to Enable the Workload View

1. Open your **Monday.com board**.
2. Click **"Views"** (top menu).
3. Select **"Workload"** from the list.
4. Click **"Add to Board"** to activate it.

■ **Now, you'll see a visual breakdown of assigned tasks per team member!**

Step 3: Customizing the Workload View

Once the Workload View is enabled, **customize it to match your project needs**.

1. Setting Up the Workload Metrics

■ **Adjust Task Duration:**

- Click **"Settings"** in the Workload View.
- Select **which column represents task duration** (e.g., **"Due Date"** or **"Start Date – End Date"**).

- Monday.com will now **distribute workload based on real task duration**.

■ **Define Task Effort:**

- Assign **a weight to each task** (e.g., **small = 1 hour, medium = 4 hours, large = 8 hours**).
- This helps track actual workload **rather than just task count**.

💡 **Tip:** If tasks vary in complexity, using task duration or effort values **provides more accurate workload tracking**.

Step 4: Identifying Overloaded Team Members

The Workload View **highlights overburdened employees in red**, making it easy to spot **who has too much work**.

1. How to Identify Overload

1. Open the **Workload View**.
2. Check for **red indicators**, showing overcapacity.
3. Click a team member's workload to **see task details**.

■ **If an employee is overloaded, reassign tasks to balance workloads!**

💡 **Use Case:** If a designer is **assigned 15 tasks while another has 5**, redistribute some work to maintain **equal productivity**.

Step 5: Reassigning Tasks for Balanced Workloads

When a team member has **too many or too few tasks**, shift assignments accordingly.

1. How to Reassign Tasks in the Workload View

1. Click on the **overloaded team member** in the Workload View.
2. Select a task that can be reassigned.
3. Click **"Change Assignee"** and select a team member with availability.
4. Confirm the reassignment.

■ **The task is now reassigned, preventing burnout and improving efficiency!**

💡 **Tip:** Use **automations** to redistribute work **dynamically based on availability**.

Step 6: Using Workload Automation

To reduce **manual adjustments**, set up **workload-based automations**.

1. Automating Workload Balancing

■ **Example Automations:**

- **"When a team member exceeds 10 tasks, auto-reassign new tasks to another team member."**
- **"If a task is marked as urgent and the assignee is at capacity, notify the project manager."**

2. How to Set Up an Automation for Workload Balancing

1. Click **"Automate"** in the board menu.
2. Choose a trigger **(e.g., "When a new task is added...")**.
3. Set an action **(e.g., "Assign to the least busy team member")**.
4. Click **"Activate"** to apply the automation.

💡 **Tip:** Use automations to **prevent last-minute workload spikes** and keep tasks evenly distributed.

Step 7: Integrating Workload View with Time Tracking

For **even more accurate workload management**, integrate the **Time Tracking Column** with the Workload View.

1. How Time Tracking Enhances Workload Management

- Displays **actual time spent vs. estimated workload**.
- Helps **refine task effort estimations**.
- Allows managers to **adjust future workloads based on real data**.

💡 **Use Case:** If **developers consistently take longer than estimated on tasks**, managers can **adjust task duration predictions for future projects**.

Step 8: Best Practices for Workload Management

⬛ **Regularly Review Workloads** – Check the Workload View **weekly** to ensure balance.
⬛ **Use Task Weights Instead of Just Task Count** – Factor in **effort level**, not just **task volume**.
⬛ **Encourage Team Members to Report Overload** – Use **pulse surveys** or meetings to gauge workload stress.
⬛ **Automate Work Redistribution** – Prevent overload **before it happens**.
⬛ **Integrate Time Tracking** – Compare **estimated vs. actual workload** for better planning.

💡 **Tip:** Conduct **monthly workload audits** to fine-tune task assignments.

Final Thoughts

The **Workload View in Monday.com** is a **powerful tool for tracking, managing, and balancing workloads** across teams. By **visualizing task distribution, automating workload balancing, and integrating time tracking**, project managers can **prevent burnout and optimize team performance**.

⬛ **You've learned how to:**

- Set up the **Workload View** to track task distribution.
- Customize workload settings **based on task duration or effort**.
- Identify **overloaded team members and redistribute tasks**.
- Use **automations to prevent work overload**.
- Integrate **time tracking for more accurate workload predictions**.

Now that you've optimized workload management, the next chapter will cover **Using Pulse for Team Health Checks**, helping you track **team well-being and engagement in Monday.com**.

Using Pulse for Team Health Checks

A successful project isn't just about **deadlines and deliverables**—it's also about ensuring that **teams remain engaged, motivated, and productive**. Without visibility into team well-being, managers risk **burnout, disengagement, and high turnover**.

Monday.com's **Pulse feature** provides a structured way to **check in on team morale, track engagement, and identify potential challenges before they escalate**.

By leveraging **Pulse for team health checks**, project managers can:
■ **Monitor team well-being** to maintain productivity and morale.
■ **Identify and address burnout risks** before they impact performance.
■ **Encourage open communication** between team members.
■ **Improve engagement by acting on feedback.**
■ **Ensure that project goals align with team capacity.**

This chapter will guide you through **setting up and using Pulse in Monday.com** to track **team health and engagement effectively**.

Step 1: Understanding Pulse in Monday.com

Pulse in Monday.com is a feature that allows managers to **collect and analyze team feedback** regarding their workload, stress levels, and engagement.

It enables teams to:

- Provide **quick status updates** on their workload and energy levels.
- Share **anonymous feedback** about project challenges.
- Report any **roadblocks affecting productivity**.

💡 **Use Case:** A project manager can run a **weekly team health check survey** to ensure that employees are **not feeling overworked or disengaged**.

Step 2: Setting Up Pulse for Your Team

1. How to Enable Pulse in Monday.com

1. Open your **Monday.com board**.
2. Click **"Views"** on the top menu.
3. Select **"Add View"** and search for **"Pulse"**.
4. Click **"Add to Board"** to activate it.

■ **Now, your team can start submitting their weekly check-ins!**

Step 3: Customizing Your Pulse Check-In

A good team health check includes **questions that reflect workload, satisfaction, and productivity**.

1. Creating Custom Pulse Questions

To get useful insights, add **relevant check-in questions**:

■ **Example Pulse Check-In Questions:**

1. **How are you feeling about your workload this week?**
   - ○ Overwhelmed
   - ○ Manageable
   - ○ Too light
2. **Do you have any roadblocks affecting your progress?**
   - ○ Yes (please specify)
   - ○ No
3. **How engaged do you feel in your current project?**
   - ○ Very engaged
   - ○ Neutral
   - ○ Disengaged
4. **Is there anything your manager can do to support you?**
   - ○ Yes (please specify)
   - ○ No, I'm good

💡 **Tip:** Keep Pulse surveys **short and simple** so that team members **don't feel burdened when responding**.

Step 4: Automating Pulse Reminders

To ensure regular check-ins, set up **automated reminders** for Pulse responses.

1. How to Set Up Weekly Pulse Reminders

1. Click **"Automate"** in the board menu.
2. Choose a trigger: **"Every Monday at 9 AM"**.
3. Select an action: **"Send a Pulse reminder to all team members."**
4. Click **"Activate"** to enable automation.

■ **Now, team members will receive a reminder to submit their check-ins!**

💡 **Use Case:** If team morale **drops consistently**, managers can **schedule one-on-one meetings** to understand concerns.

Step 5: Analyzing Pulse Results

Once Pulse check-ins are collected, use Monday.com's **dashboard features** to analyze trends.

1. How to View Pulse Analytics

1. Click on the **Pulse View** in your board.
2. Navigate to **"Analytics"** to see response trends.
3. Filter by **week, department, or team member** to identify patterns.
4. Export the data as a report if needed.

■ **Key Metrics to Track in Pulse Reports:**

- **Overall team morale** over time.
- **Workload balance trends.**
- **Frequency of reported roadblocks.**

Tip: If multiple employees report feeling **overwhelmed**, consider **adjusting workloads or extending deadlines**.

Step 6: Taking Action Based on Pulse Insights

Pulse is **only effective if managers act on the data**. Once results are analyzed, take **proactive steps** to improve team well-being.

1. Addressing Overwork or Low Morale

If the majority of the team feels overworked:

- Redistribute tasks using the **Workload View**.
- Extend project deadlines if necessary.
- Encourage breaks and time-off to prevent burnout.

If employees report feeling disengaged:

- Offer more **ownership and responsibility** in projects.
- Recognize achievements **through public appreciation**.
- Conduct **team-building activities or workshops**.

If specific roadblocks keep appearing in Pulse responses:

- Schedule a **team meeting to discuss solutions**.
- Assign a **dedicated project lead to resolve key challenges**.
- Offer **more resources or training** if needed.

Use Case: If multiple employees report **"Too many meetings"**, reduce unnecessary calls and switch to **asynchronous updates**.

Step 7: Best Practices for Effective Team Health Checks

Keep Pulse Check-Ins Short and Simple – Avoid overwhelming team members with long surveys.
Encourage Honest Feedback – Allow **anonymous responses** for more candid insights.
Analyze Trends Over Time – Don't just look at one week's responses; track **patterns across months**.
Follow Up on Concerns – If employees report **issues, act quickly to address them**.
Balance Workload Proactively – Use **Pulse insights + Workload View** to prevent burnout.

Tip: Run **quarterly engagement reviews** based on Pulse reports to continuously improve team morale.

Final Thoughts

Using **Pulse for team health checks** in Monday.com allows managers to **monitor engagement, reduce burnout, and foster a more productive work environment**. By **tracking morale, identifying workload concerns, and acting on feedback**, teams can remain **highly engaged and efficient**.

You've learned how to:

- Set up **Pulse for team check-ins**.

- Customize **Pulse questions for meaningful insights**.
- Automate **weekly check-in reminders**.
- Analyze **team health data for trends**.
- Take **action based on Pulse feedback**.

Now that you've mastered **team health tracking**, the next chapter will cover **Advanced Filters and Search for Data Insights**, helping you **organize and retrieve critical project data quickly in Monday.com**.

Advanced Filters and Search for Data Insights

As projects grow in complexity, managing **large amounts of data efficiently** becomes crucial for project managers. Without a structured way to **filter and search for information**, teams risk **wasting time navigating boards, missing deadlines, and overlooking critical tasks**.

Monday.com offers **powerful filtering and search tools** that allow project managers to:
■ **Quickly locate tasks, documents, and communications.**
■ **Apply advanced filters to display only relevant data.**
■ **Save custom views for different project needs.**
■ **Extract insights by combining search and filtering features.**
■ **Enhance team efficiency by eliminating clutter.**

This chapter will guide you through **using Monday.com's advanced filters and search capabilities** to **improve data retrieval and project visibility**.

Step 1: Understanding Advanced Filters

Filters in Monday.com allow you to **display only the most relevant information** by **applying conditions to your data**.

1. How to Use Filters in Monday.com

1. Open a **Monday.com board** where you manage tasks.
2. Click on the **Filter button** (funnel icon) at the top of your board.
3. Choose filter criteria (e.g., **Status, Due Date, Priority, Assignee**).
4. The board updates in real time to show only **items that meet the filter conditions**.

■ **Example Filters:**

- Show **only tasks assigned to you**.
- Display **all overdue tasks**.
- View **only high-priority tasks for this week**.

💡 **Use Case:** A project manager can **filter the board to show only "Pending Approval" tasks assigned to the marketing team** to prioritize work.

Step 2: Creating Custom Filtered Views

Rather than **applying filters manually every time**, you can **save custom filtered views** for quick access.

1. How to Save a Custom View with Filters

1. Apply the desired filters to your board.
2. Click **"Save as New View."**
3. Name the view (e.g., **"Urgent Tasks" or "This Week's Deadlines"**).
4. Now, the view is available in the **Views dropdown menu**.

■ **Examples of Custom Views:**

- **"High-Priority Tasks"** → Shows only **urgent and high-priority items**.
- **"Weekly Work Summary"** → Displays all tasks **due this week**.

- "Completed Projects" → Filters tasks where the **status is marked as "Done"**.

🔔 **Use Case:** Instead of manually filtering **each morning**, a team lead can **create a saved view for daily stand-up meetings**.

Step 3: Using Search Everything for Quick Data Retrieval

Monday.com's **Search Everything feature** allows users to **quickly find any data across all boards, files, and updates**.

1. How to Use Search Everything

1. Click on the **search bar** at the top of Monday.com.
2. Enter keywords related to what you're looking for.
3. Filter search results by **board, team, or timeframe**.

🔲 **Examples of Useful Searches:**

- **Find all tasks assigned to a specific person.**
- **Locate a document shared in a past update.**
- **Retrieve all conversations mentioning a project.**
- **Search for completed tasks from last quarter.**

🔔 **Use Case:** If a team member asks about a **proposal document shared last month**, use **Search Everything** to find it instantly instead of scrolling through updates.

Step 4: Combining Filters and Search for Deeper Insights

For **more advanced data retrieval**, combine **Filters + Search Everything**.

1. Example Workflows:

🔲 **To find urgent sales leads** →

- Filter by **Priority: High** + Search for "Sales Lead".

🔲 **To review all design feedback this month** →

- Filter by **Team: Design** + Search for "Feedback" **+ Date Range: Last 30 Days**.

🔲 **To identify overdue software bug fixes** →

- Filter by **Status: Not Completed** + Search for "Bug Fix".

🔔 **Tip:** This approach ensures you **always find the most relevant data quickly**.

Step 5: Automating Data Insights with Advanced Filters

Monday.com allows users to **automate workflows based on filter results**.

1. How to Set Up Automations for Filtered Data

1. Click **"Automate"** on your board.

2. Select a trigger **(e.g., "When a high-priority task is created...")**.
3. Set an action **(e.g., "...Notify the project manager immediately.")**.
4. Click **"Activate"** to enable automation.

■ **Example Automations Using Filters:**

- **"When a deadline is within 48 hours, send a Slack notification."**
- **"When a new task is tagged as 'Urgent,' assign it to the team lead."**
- **"When a completed project is archived, generate a report."**

💡 **Use Case:** If a project manager wants to **be alerted when an urgent task is due soon**, an automation can **filter and notify them in real-time**.

Step 6: Using Filters and Search for Reporting

Advanced filtering and search can help **generate better reports** by extracting **only relevant data**.

1. How to Generate Reports Using Filters

1. Apply filters to **narrow down the dataset**.
2. Export the filtered view as **CSV or Excel**.
3. Use external reporting tools (Google Sheets, Power BI) **for deeper analysis**.

■ **Example Reports You Can Create:**

- **Monthly Performance Report** → Filter by **Completed Tasks + Date Range**.
- **Resource Allocation Report** → Filter by **Team Member + Assigned Workload**.
- **Risk Assessment Report** → Filter by **Overdue + High Priority Tasks**.

💡 **Tip:** Combine **filtered data + time tracking reports** to analyze **productivity trends**.

Step 7: Best Practices for Filtering and Search

■ **Use Filters for Quick Insights** – Avoid manually sorting through data.
■ **Save Custom Views** – Set up **pre-filtered views** for commonly used reports.
■ **Automate Workflows Based on Filters** – Get **real-time alerts for key updates**.
■ **Use Search Everything for Deep Data Retrieval** – Find **specific tasks, files, and updates instantly**.
■ **Export Filtered Reports** – Generate reports **for leadership and clients**.

💡 **Tip:** Review **filtered views weekly** to ensure you're tracking the right insights.

Final Thoughts

Advanced filtering and search capabilities in Monday.com empower project managers to retrieve critical data efficiently, optimize workflows, and improve team productivity. By leveraging **custom views, search functions, and automation**, project teams can **streamline project tracking and decision-making**.

■ **You've learned how to:**

- Apply **filters to display only relevant project data**.

- Create **custom views for recurring use cases**.
- Use **Search Everything to retrieve files, tasks, and updates**.
- Automate workflows **based on filtered data**.
- Generate **insightful reports using filters and exports**.

Now that you've optimized **data retrieval and reporting**, the next chapter will cover **Connecting Monday.com to Email and Calendar Tools**, helping you **streamline communication and scheduling directly within Monday.com**.

Section 7:
Integrations and Extensions

Connecting Monday.com to Email and Calendar Tools

Effective project management requires **seamless communication and scheduling**. By integrating Monday.com with **email and calendar tools**, teams can:
■ **Sync project deadlines with their calendars** for better time management.
■ **Receive task updates via email** without needing to check Monday.com constantly.
■ **Automate notifications** to ensure no deadlines are missed.
■ **Centralize project-related communication** directly within Monday.com.

In this chapter, we'll explore **how to connect Monday.com to email and calendar tools like Gmail, Outlook, and Google Calendar** to enhance productivity and collaboration.

Step 1: Connecting Monday.com to Your Email

Monday.com integrates with **Gmail, Outlook, and other email providers** to streamline communication. This integration allows teams to:

- **Receive email notifications for important updates**.
- **Create tasks from emails automatically**.
- **Reply to comments and updates directly from email**.

1. How to Connect Monday.com to Gmail or Outlook

1. Go to **Monday.com** and open the **Integrations Center**.
2. Search for **"Gmail"** or **"Outlook"**.
3. Click **"Add Integration"** and follow the authentication steps.
4. Once connected, set up automation rules **(e.g., "When an email arrives, create a task in Monday.com")**.

■ **Now, you can send and receive Monday.com updates via email!**

Step 2: Automating Email Notifications

To ensure **important updates reach the right people**, automate email notifications for:
■ **New task assignments**
■ **Status changes (e.g., task moved to "Urgent")**
■ **Upcoming deadlines**

1. Setting Up Automated Email Alerts

1. Open your **Monday.com board**.
2. Click **"Automate"** > **"Create Automation"**.

3. Choose a trigger **(e.g., "When a due date is approaching…")**.
4. Select an action **(e.g., "Send an email to the task owner")**.
5. Save the automation.

💡 **Use Case:** If a deadline is **two days away**, an automatic **email reminder is sent** to the responsible team member.

Step 3: Syncing Monday.com with Google Calendar

Monday.com can sync with **Google Calendar** so that tasks, deadlines, and events appear in a **single view**.

1. How to Connect Monday.com to Google Calendar

1. Open your **Monday.com board**.
2. Click **"Integrations"** > **"Google Calendar"**.
3. Select **"Sync items with Google Calendar"**.
4. Choose the **date column** (e.g., **Due Date**) for calendar syncing.
5. Click **"Add to Calendar"** and confirm.

⬛ **Now, Monday.com tasks appear in your Google Calendar!**

💡 **Tip:** Use color-coding in Google Calendar to **differentiate project deadlines from personal events**.

Step 4: Syncing Monday.com with Outlook Calendar

For Outlook users, syncing Monday.com ensures that **deadlines and meetings appear in one place**.

1. How to Sync Monday.com with Outlook Calendar

1. Open your **Monday.com board**.
2. Click **"Integrations"** > **"Outlook Calendar"**.
3. Select **"Sync tasks with Outlook"**.
4. Choose the **date column to sync** (e.g., Due Date, Meeting Date).
5. Confirm integration and **enable two-way syncing if needed**.

⬛ **Now, all Monday.com deadlines are reflected in Outlook!**

💡 **Tip:** Set up Outlook notifications to **remind you of upcoming Monday.com tasks**.

Step 5: Creating Tasks from Emails Automatically

Rather than manually creating tasks, you can **convert emails into Monday.com tasks automatically**.

1. Automating Task Creation from Emails

1. In **Monday.com**, go to **"Integrations"** > **"Email"**.
2. Select **Gmail or Outlook**.
3. Set a rule: **"When an email arrives with the subject 'New Task'…"**
4. Choose an action: **"Create a new task in Monday.com"**.
5. Assign the task to a team member automatically.

■ **Now, project-related emails turn into tasks without manual entry!**

💡 **Use Case:** If a client sends an email with **"Urgent Task"** in the subject, Monday.com **automatically creates a task and assigns it to the right team member**.

Step 6: Best Practices for Email and Calendar Integrations

■ **Enable two-way syncing** – Ensure Monday.com tasks **update in real-time** in your calendar.
■ **Use email filtering** – Prevent clutter by filtering out **non-urgent notifications**.
■ **Set reminders for deadlines** – Sync deadlines with **Google/Outlook notifications**.
■ **Automate repetitive emails** – Convert client requests into **Monday.com tasks** instantly.
■ **Regularly review calendar sync settings** – Ensure all **projects are accurately reflected**.

💡 **Tip:** For teams managing multiple projects, **create a dedicated "Monday.com Calendar"** in Google/Outlook to keep work and personal events separate.

Final Thoughts

Integrating Monday.com with email and calendar tools enhances **workflow efficiency, improves task tracking, and ensures no deadlines are missed**. By automating notifications, syncing deadlines, and creating tasks directly from emails, project managers can **eliminate manual follow-ups and streamline project execution**.

■ **You've learned how to:**

- **Connect Monday.com to Gmail and Outlook** for seamless email communication.
- **Automate email notifications** for important updates.
- **Sync tasks with Google and Outlook Calendar** for better scheduling.
- **Create Monday.com tasks from emails automatically.**

Now that you've integrated Monday.com with **email and calendar tools**, the next chapter will cover **Syncing Monday.com with Cloud Storage (Google Drive, Dropbox, etc.)**, helping you manage **project files efficiently**.

Syncing with Cloud Storage (Google Drive, Dropbox)

Effective project management relies on **seamless access to documents, spreadsheets, and media files**. Syncing Monday.com with **Google Drive, Dropbox, and other cloud storage services** ensures that teams can:

■ **Store and access files directly from Monday.com** without switching platforms.
■ **Automatically attach relevant documents to tasks** for better organization.
■ **Enable real-time collaboration on shared documents**.
■ **Reduce file duplication and version control issues**.
■ **Securely store important project files** in one centralized location.

This chapter will guide you through **integrating Monday.com with Google Drive and Dropbox**, along with best practices for managing files efficiently.

Step 1: Connecting Google Drive to Monday.com

Google Drive is one of the most widely used cloud storage services. **Integrating it with Monday.com** allows you to attach and manage documents within your workflow.

1. How to Connect Google Drive to Monday.com

1. Open your **Monday.com board**.
2. Click on a **task (item) where you want to attach a document**.
3. Click the **"Files" column** and select **"Google Drive"**.
4. Authenticate your Google account.
5. Select a file from Google Drive and click **"Attach"**.

■ **Now, the file is directly linked to the task, and team members can access it instantly!**

💡 **Use Case:** If a marketing team is working on a campaign, they can **attach design assets, content drafts, and presentations from Google Drive directly to Monday.com tasks**.

Step 2: Connecting Dropbox to Monday.com

Dropbox provides **secure cloud storage and file-sharing capabilities**. Syncing it with Monday.com enables teams to **attach and organize files easily**.

1. How to Connect Dropbox to Monday.com

1. Open your **Monday.com board**.
2. Click on a task and navigate to the **Files column**.
3. Select **"Dropbox"** and log in to your account.
4. Choose the file you want to attach and click **"Link"**.

■ **Now, the file is accessible within Monday.com and can be opened anytime.**

💡 **Use Case:** A software development team can **attach product specifications, test reports, and code documentation stored in Dropbox to corresponding Monday.com tasks**.

Step 3: Automating File Management with Integrations

Monday.com's **automations** allow teams to automatically **attach, organize, and update files** based on specific triggers.

1. Automating File Attachments

1. Click **"Automate"** on your Monday.com board.
2. Select a trigger: **"When a new task is created…"**
3. Set an action: **"Attach a file from Google Drive/Dropbox."**
4. Choose a **default folder** where files should be saved.
5. Click **"Activate"** to enable automation.

■ Now, files are attached automatically to newly created tasks!

💡 Use Case: A content team can **automatically attach a template document from Google Drive whenever a new article task is created**.

Step 4: Using Cloud Storage for Version Control

Version control is crucial to prevent **overwriting or losing important file updates**.

1. Best Practices for Version Control in Monday.com

■ **Enable Google Drive's version history** – Track changes to documents over time.
■ **Label files clearly (e.g., v1, v2, final version)** – Prevent confusion.
■ **Use Dropbox's "File Request" feature** – Collect updated files from team members efficiently.
■ **Store important project milestones in a dedicated cloud folder** – Archive completed files securely.

💡 Use Case: A design team can use **Google Drive's version control to track edits on creative assets attached to Monday.com tasks**.

Step 5: Managing File Access and Permissions

To maintain **data security and collaboration efficiency**, it's essential to **manage access permissions** properly.

1. How to Manage File Access in Google Drive

1. Open the file in Google Drive.
2. Click **"Share"**.
3. Select **access levels** (Viewer, Commenter, Editor).
4. Set expiration dates for temporary access if needed.
5. Click **"Copy Link"** and attach it to the corresponding Monday.com task.

💡 Tip: Restrict access to confidential files while allowing broader collaboration on shared documents.

2. How to Manage File Access in Dropbox

1. Right-click the file in Dropbox.
2. Click **"Share"**.
3. Choose whether people **can edit or only view the file**.
4. Set a password for extra security.
5. Attach the file link to Monday.com.

■ Now, team members can access only the files relevant to them.

💡 **Use Case:** A finance team can **store financial reports in Dropbox and grant view-only access to project stakeholders through Monday.com**.

Step 6: Using File Search and Filters for Easy Retrieval

When managing **multiple files across projects**, it's crucial to **retrieve them quickly**.

1. How to Search for Files in Monday.com

1. Use **Monday.com's "Search Everything"** feature.
2. Type the **file name, document title, or keyword**.
3. Filter by **board, project, or date**.

■ Now, all related files will appear instantly.

💡 **Use Case:** If a project manager needs a **contract uploaded last month**, they can use the search function instead of manually checking each task.

Step 7: Best Practices for Syncing Cloud Storage with Monday.com

■ **Organize files by project** – Use dedicated **Google Drive or Dropbox folders** for each project.
■ **Automate file attachments** – Reduce manual uploads by linking cloud storage with **Monday.com automations**.
■ **Maintain version control** – Use **file history tracking** to manage document revisions.
■ **Limit access to sensitive files** – Use **Google Drive's permission settings** to control **who can edit, comment, or view**.
■ **Regularly clean up old files** – Archive or remove outdated documents to keep **storage organized**.

💡 **Tip:** Use **Monday.com's File Column** to track which files are attached to each task for **better visibility**.

Final Thoughts

Integrating Monday.com with Google Drive and Dropbox significantly improves **file accessibility, collaboration, and project efficiency**. By keeping all **important documents linked to tasks**, teams can eliminate **file duplication, reduce time spent searching for information, and enhance workflow management**.

■ **You've learned how to:**

- **Connect Google Drive and Dropbox to Monday.com** for seamless file management.
- **Automate file uploads and attachments** for efficient project tracking.
- **Use version control and access permissions** to keep data secure.
- **Search and filter files** for quick retrieval.

Now that you've optimized **file management in Monday.com**, the next chapter will cover **CRM and Marketing Tool Integrations**, helping you streamline **client management and marketing workflows** within Monday.com.

CRM and Marketing Tool Integrations

Managing customer relationships and marketing campaigns efficiently is essential for business success. Integrating **Customer Relationship Management (CRM) and marketing tools** with Monday.com enables teams to:

■ **Streamline lead tracking and sales pipelines**
■ **Automate marketing workflows**
■ **Improve customer communication and engagement**
■ **Gain better insights with data-driven reporting**
■ **Reduce time spent switching between multiple platforms**

Monday.com integrates with **popular CRM and marketing platforms** such as **HubSpot, Salesforce, Mailchimp, ActiveCampaign, and Facebook Ads**, making it an all-in-one solution for sales and marketing teams.

Step 1: Connecting Monday.com to a CRM Platform

CRM integrations allow businesses to **track leads, manage sales pipelines, and maintain customer relationships** directly from Monday.com.

1. How to Connect Monday.com to HubSpot CRM

1. Open **Monday.com** and navigate to the **Integrations Center**.
2. Search for **"HubSpot"** and select **"Connect"**.
3. Authenticate your **HubSpot account** and allow permissions.
4. Choose automation rules, such as:
   - **"When a new deal is created in HubSpot, add it as an item in Monday.com."**
   - **"When a deal is updated in HubSpot, reflect the change in Monday.com."**
5. Click **"Activate"** to complete the integration.

■ **Now, HubSpot deals, contacts, and company details sync automatically with Monday.com.**

💡 **Use Case:** A sales team can **track and manage their entire pipeline in Monday.com while keeping customer data updated via HubSpot.**

Step 2: Connecting Monday.com to Salesforce

Salesforce is a **widely used CRM for managing customer relationships and tracking deals**. Integrating it with Monday.com enables teams to **sync leads, opportunities, and customer records**.

1. How to Connect Monday.com to Salesforce

1. Open **Monday.com's Integrations Center**.
2. Search for **"Salesforce"** and click **"Connect"**.
3. Authenticate your **Salesforce account**.
4. Select an automation, such as:
   - **"When a new lead is added in Salesforce, create a task in Monday.com."**
   - **"When a deal is closed in Salesforce, update the corresponding task in Monday.com."**
5. Click **"Save & Activate"**.

■ **Now, Monday.com and Salesforce are fully synchronized, reducing manual data entry.**

💡 **Use Case:** A business development team can **monitor Salesforce leads and their progress in Monday.com boards, ensuring smooth collaboration between sales and project teams**.

Step 3: Integrating Email Marketing Tools (Mailchimp, ActiveCampaign)

Email marketing platforms like **Mailchimp and ActiveCampaign** help businesses automate email campaigns, manage subscribers, and analyze campaign performance.

1. How to Connect Mailchimp to Monday.com

1. Open **Monday.com's Integrations Center**.
2. Search for **"Mailchimp"** and select **"Connect"**.
3. Authenticate your **Mailchimp account**.
4. Choose automations, such as:
    - **"When a new subscriber is added in Mailchimp, create a task in Monday.com."**
    - **"When an email campaign is sent, update the status in Monday.com."**
5. Click **"Activate"** to complete the integration.

■ **Now, marketing teams can track subscriber activity and email campaigns inside Monday.com.**

💡 **Use Case:** A marketing team can **automate follow-ups based on Mailchimp email engagement, triggering tasks in Monday.com when leads show interest**.

Step 4: Managing Paid Ad Campaigns (Facebook Ads, Google Ads)

Tracking the performance of **Facebook Ads and Google Ads** campaigns directly in Monday.com allows marketing teams to **monitor results and adjust strategies efficiently**.

1. How to Integrate Facebook Ads with Monday.com

1. Go to **Monday.com's Integrations Center**.
2. Search for **"Facebook Ads"** and select **"Connect"**.
3. Authenticate your **Facebook Business account**.
4. Set up automations, such as:
    - **"When a new lead is generated from a Facebook Ad, create a task in Monday.com."**
    - **"When a campaign reaches a milestone, notify the marketing team."**
5. Click **"Activate"**.

■ **Now, Facebook Ads lead data syncs automatically with Monday.com.**

💡 **Use Case:** A digital marketing team can **track ad spend, campaign conversions, and lead generation directly from Monday.com**.

Step 5: Automating CRM and Marketing Workflows

Monday.com allows teams to **automate repetitive marketing and CRM tasks**, ensuring efficiency and consistency.

1. Automating Lead Management

1. Click **"Automate"** on your Monday.com board.
2. Select a trigger: **"When a new lead is added in CRM…"**

3. Set an action: **"Assign it to a sales representative in Monday.com."**
4. Click **"Save & Activate."**

■ Now, leads are automatically assigned to sales reps, reducing response times.

♥ **Use Case:** A customer support team can **trigger follow-ups in Monday.com when a lead is marked as "Interested" in Salesforce.**

Step 6: Tracking CRM and Marketing Performance

Monday.com's **dashboards and reporting tools** allow teams to **track key performance indicators (KPIs),** such as:

■ **Number of new leads per week**
■ **Conversion rates from marketing campaigns**
■ **Customer retention trends**
■ **Email campaign open and click-through rates**

1. How to Create a Performance Dashboard in Monday.com

1. Click **"Dashboards" > "Create New Dashboard".**
2. Add widgets such as:
   ○ **CRM Sales Funnel** – Track lead progress.
   ○ **Campaign Performance Chart** – Monitor email and ad effectiveness.
   ○ **Sales Rep Performance** – Compare deal closures across team members.
3. Save and **share the dashboard with stakeholders.**

■ Now, all CRM and marketing metrics are easily accessible in Monday.com.

♥ **Use Case:** A marketing manager can **review the success of campaigns and make data-driven decisions using Monday.com reports.**

Best Practices for CRM & Marketing Tool Integrations

■ **Automate lead tracking** – Reduce manual data entry by syncing CRM tools.
■ **Centralize marketing data** – Keep campaign performance data in Monday.com.
■ **Assign leads efficiently** – Use Monday.com's automations for faster follow-ups.
■ **Monitor campaign ROI** – Track ad performance and budget utilization.
■ **Ensure seamless collaboration** – Enable sales, marketing, and customer support teams to access real-time data.

♥ **Tip:** Use **Monday.com's automation recipes** to trigger **reminders, notifications, and task updates** based on CRM and marketing activity.

Final Thoughts

Integrating Monday.com with CRM and marketing tools improves **lead tracking, campaign efficiency, and customer engagement**. By automating tasks and centralizing data, teams can focus on **driving conversions and optimizing marketing efforts**.

■ You've learned how to:

- **Connect Monday.com to HubSpot and Salesforce CRM** for lead tracking.
- **Sync with Mailchimp for email marketing automation.**
- **Manage Facebook Ads and Google Ads campaign performance.**
- **Automate lead assignments and sales follow-ups.**
- **Track marketing and sales KPIs with dashboards.**

Now that your **CRM and marketing tools are integrated**, the next chapter will cover **Leveraging the Monday.com API for Custom Solutions**, helping you **customize and extend Monday.com's capabilities**.

Leveraging the Monday.com API for Custom Solutions

Monday.com is a powerful **no-code/low-code** project management platform, but for businesses with **unique workflows, deeper integrations, or custom automation needs**, the **Monday.com API** provides the flexibility to:

■ **Connect Monday.com with internal business systems**
■ **Automate repetitive tasks beyond built-in automations**
■ **Pull data from Monday.com for external reporting and analysis**
■ **Create custom dashboards and workflows**
■ **Integrate with proprietary software or industry-specific tools**

This chapter will guide you through **how to use the Monday.com API**, including authentication, common use cases, and best practices for development.

Step 1: Understanding the Monday.com API

Monday.com provides a **GraphQL-based API**, which allows developers to **fetch, modify, and update data efficiently**.

1. What Can You Do with the API?

With the Monday.com API, you can:

* **Retrieve board and item data** (e.g., projects, tasks, updates)
* **Create, update, and delete boards and tasks dynamically**
* **Automate workflows by connecting Monday.com to other platforms**
* **Trigger actions based on external events**
* **Customize reporting by extracting data for business intelligence tools**

Step 2: Setting Up API Access

To start using the API, you need an **API key** from Monday.com.

1. How to Generate Your API Key

1. Go to **Monday.com** and navigate to your **Admin settings**.
2. Click on **"API" or "Developers"**.
3. Generate a **personal API token** or create an **OAuth app** for enterprise use.
4. Save the API key securely (never share it publicly).

💡 **Tip:** If you are developing integrations for multiple teams, use **OAuth authentication** instead of personal API tokens.

Step 3: Making API Requests

Since Monday.com uses **GraphQL**, you can send queries using **cURL, Postman, or any programming language (Python, JavaScript, etc.)**.

1. Example: Fetching All Boards

```
query {
  boards {
    id
    name
    items {
      id
      name
    }
  }
}
```

📌 This request retrieves all boards along with their item (task) details.

2. Example: Creating a New Task in a Board

```
mutation {
  create_item(
    board_id: 123456789,
    item_name: "New Task",
    column_values: "{ \"status\": \"Working on it\" }"
  ) {
    id
  }
}
```

📌 This mutation creates a new task with the status "Working on it."

Step 4: Integrating Monday.com API with External Tools

Many businesses integrate Monday.com with their **CRM, ERP, or financial systems** using the API.

1. Connecting Monday.com to an Internal CRM

Example: Automatically create a task in Monday.com when a **new lead** is added to a CRM.

- Set up a **Webhook in your CRM** (e.g., HubSpot, Salesforce).
- Trigger an API request to **create a new Monday.com item** when a lead is added.
- Assign the lead to a **sales team member** and track follow-ups.

📌 Now, sales reps see new leads as tasks in Monday.com without manual entry.

Step 5: Automating Workflows Beyond Built-in Automations

Monday.com offers **native automation recipes**, but some businesses need **advanced custom workflows**.

1. Automating Task Status Based on External Events

Example: If a **support ticket is resolved in Zendesk**, update the corresponding task in Monday.com.

1. **Set up a webhook in Zendesk** to listen for ticket resolution.

2. **Trigger a Monday.com API call** to update the task status.
3. **Send notifications to project stakeholders** automatically.

📌 This eliminates the need for manual task updates in Monday.com.

Step 6: Extracting Monday.com Data for Reports & Dashboards

Monday.com provides **native dashboards**, but businesses needing **advanced reporting** can export data via API.

1. Pulling Monday.com Data into Google Sheets for Analysis

Example: Fetch **weekly task completion reports** and send them to Google Sheets.

- Use **Google Apps Script** or Python to query Monday.com API.
- Extract **task completion rates, overdue tasks, and project summaries**.
- Automate **weekly report generation** in Google Sheets or Power BI.

📌 This allows managers to analyze productivity trends beyond Monday.com's built-in dashboards.

Step 7: Building Custom Applications with the Monday.com API

For businesses that require **custom applications**, the Monday.com API allows developers to create:

- **Custom client portals** – Allow external clients to view project progress without full Monday.com access.
- **Automated billing workflows** – Sync Monday.com tasks with invoicing software.
- **AI-driven task management** – Use AI tools (e.g., ChatGPT, Zapier AI) to suggest task priorities.

📌 **Example:** A law firm can build a **custom legal case management dashboard** using Monday.com's API to track client cases, deadlines, and documents.

Best Practices for Using the Monday.com API

🔳 **Use OAuth for Enterprise Integrations** – Secure your API access with proper authentication.
🔳 **Optimize API Queries** – Only fetch **necessary data** to improve performance.
🔳 **Implement Rate Limiting** – Monday.com has **API rate limits**, so optimize requests.
🔳 **Secure API Keys** – Store them in **environment variables**, not in source code.
🔳 **Use Webhooks for Real-Time Updates** – Reduce polling and receive event-driven notifications.

💡 **Tip:** Use **Postman or GraphQL Playground** to test API queries before deploying in production.

Final Thoughts

The **Monday.com API unlocks endless possibilities** for teams needing **custom integrations, workflow automation, and data-driven decision-making**. Whether you're **connecting CRM systems, automating business processes, or extracting insights**, the API enables **powerful enhancements** beyond Monday.com's native capabilities.

■ You've learned how to:

- **Set up and authenticate API access** in Monday.com.
- **Query, create, and update data** using GraphQL.
- **Integrate Monday.com with external CRM and business tools**.
- **Automate workflows beyond built-in features**.
- **Extract and visualize data** for better reporting.

Now that you've explored **custom integrations with the Monday.com API**, the next section will cover **Best Practices and Pitfalls to Avoid**, ensuring your Monday.com usage remains **efficient, secure, and scalable**.

Section 8:
Best Practices and Pitfalls to Avoid

Top 10 Tips for Optimizing Monday.com

Monday.com is a **powerful project management tool**, but to get the most out of it, you need to **optimize your workflows, boards, and team collaboration**. An inefficient setup can lead to **cluttered boards, redundant tasks, and poor visibility**, whereas an optimized system ensures **productivity, clarity, and efficiency**.

Below are the **top 10 tips** to optimize Monday.com for your projects and teams.

---

1. Use Clear and Consistent Naming Conventions

One of the biggest pitfalls in Monday.com is **confusing board, group, and item names**. Establishing a **consistent naming structure** helps everyone quickly identify projects, tasks, and statuses.

■ Best Practice:

- Use a **standardized naming format** for boards, such as:
    - [Department] - [Project Name] - [Year/Quarter]
    - Example: **Marketing - Website Redesign - Q2 2025**
- For tasks, use **clear action-oriented names** like:
    - "Finalize Budget Proposal" instead of "Budget"
    - "Update Sales Report for Q1" instead of "Sales Report"

- **Benefit:** Reduces confusion and helps users quickly locate and organize tasks.

---

2. Customize Columns for Maximum Efficiency

Monday.com provides **various column types** (Status, Timeline, Formula, Dropdown, etc.), but many teams **don't fully utilize them**.

■ Best Practice:

- Use **Status Columns** for task progress (To Do, In Progress, Done).
- Add a **Priority Column** to identify urgent tasks.
- Use the **Timeline or Date Column** to set deadlines.
- Utilize **Formula Columns** to calculate progress, costs, or custom metrics.

- **Benefit:** Customizing columns makes it easier to track **task status, deadlines, and priorities at a glance**.

---

3. Automate Repetitive Tasks

Monday.com's **automation recipes** help **eliminate manual work** and ensure nothing falls through the cracks.

◼ Best Practice:

- **Move tasks automatically** when status changes (e.g., "When status changes to Done, move item to Completed group").
- **Send notifications** when a deadline is approaching (e.g., "Notify the team 3 days before the due date").
- **Assign team members automatically** based on specific conditions (e.g., "If priority is High, assign to Project Manager").

- ◆ **Benefit:** Reduces **manual workload**, increases **efficiency**, and ensures **tasks flow smoothly**.

---

4. Utilize Dashboards for Real-Time Insights

Monday.com's **dashboards** allow you to see project progress, workloads, and key metrics at a glance.

◼ Best Practice:

- Use **Progress Tracking Widgets** to monitor completion rates.
- Set up **Workload View** to balance tasks across your team.
- Use **Gantt Chart View** to visualize dependencies and timelines.
- Add a **Time Tracking Widget** to measure productivity.

- ◆ **Benefit:** Provides **instant visibility into project health**, team workload, and bottlenecks.

---

5. Keep Boards Clean & Organized

A messy board can make project management **chaotic**. A well-structured board improves **focus and navigation**.

◼ Best Practice:

- **Archive** completed projects instead of deleting them.
- Use **Groups** to segment tasks by **phases, sprints, or teams**.
- **Remove unused columns** to declutter views.
- **Use board permissions** to control access levels and prevent accidental changes.

- ◆ **Benefit:** Keeps your workspace **organized, easy to navigate, and free from clutter**.

---

6. Leverage Integrations for Seamless Workflows

Monday.com integrates with various **third-party tools** like **Slack, Google Drive, Zapier, Zoom, Trello, and CRM systems**.

◼ Best Practice:

- **Sync Google Drive or Dropbox** to attach files directly to tasks.
- **Use Slack integration** to receive task updates in your Slack channels.
- **Connect Monday.com with CRM tools** (Salesforce, HubSpot) for seamless lead tracking.
- **Use Zapier to automate data transfer** between Monday.com and other apps.

- Benefit: Reduces **manual data entry** and ensures **real-time synchronization** with your existing tools.

---

7. Optimize Workload Management

To prevent **overloading team members**, use Monday.com's **Workload View** to balance task distribution.

Best Practice:

- Assign **time estimates** to each task.
- Use the **Workload Widget** to ensure no team member is overwhelmed.
- **Reassign tasks dynamically** when one team member is overloaded.

- Benefit: Helps **balance workloads**, ensuring **team efficiency and well-being**.

---

8. Use Templates for Faster Project Setup

If you frequently create similar projects, **templates save time and ensure consistency**.

Best Practice:

- **Create reusable board templates** for common projects.
- Use **pre-built Monday.com templates** for project management, marketing, HR, or IT.
- **Customize templates** with standard task lists, columns, and automations.

- Benefit: Reduces setup time and **ensures best practices are applied** to every project.

---

9. Enable Real-Time Collaboration Features

Monday.com provides **real-time collaboration tools** such as **comments, file sharing, and mentions** to enhance teamwork.

Best Practice:

- Use **@mentions** to notify team members in task updates.
- Keep all **project-related files and discussions** in the task comments.
- Use the **Updates section** instead of email chains to track communication.

- Benefit: Keeps **all team discussions, feedback, and documents centralized**.

---

10. Regularly Review and Optimize Your Workflow

Monday.com is **continuously evolving**, and so should your workflow. Regularly review **how your team is using it** and make adjustments.

Best Practice:

- Conduct **quarterly reviews** of boards and automation effectiveness.
- Gather **team feedback** on workflow improvements.
- Stay updated on **Monday.com's new features and integrations**.
- Regularly **archive outdated boards** to maintain a clean workspace.

* **Benefit:** Ensures that your **Monday.com setup stays efficient and aligned with evolving team needs**.

Final Thoughts

Optimizing Monday.com is **not just about using its features but using them strategically** to create a **seamless workflow** that enhances **team collaboration and efficiency**.

Quick Recap of Optimization Tips:

- ◼ **Use clear naming conventions**
- ◼ **Customize columns for better tracking**
- ◼ **Automate repetitive tasks**
- ◼ **Leverage dashboards for insights**
- ◼ **Keep boards organized and decluttered**
- ◼ **Integrate with other tools** for smooth workflows
- ◼ **Manage workloads efficiently**
- ◼ **Use templates to save time**
- ◼ **Enable real-time collaboration tools**
- ◼ **Review and improve workflows regularly**

Now that you've mastered optimization, the next chapter explores **Common Mistakes New Users Make (and How to Fix Them)**—so you can **avoid pitfalls and get the most out of Monday.com**.

Common Mistakes New Users Make (and How to Fix Them)

Monday.com is a **versatile and powerful project management tool**, but like any software, **new users often make common mistakes** that hinder productivity. These mistakes can lead to **disorganized boards, inefficient workflows, and reduced team collaboration**. The good news? These mistakes are **easily avoidable** with the right approach.

In this chapter, we'll explore **the most common mistakes** new users make and provide **practical solutions** to optimize your Monday.com experience.

---

1. Overcomplicating Boards with Too Many Columns

■ **The Mistake:**
New users tend to **overload boards with excessive columns**, thinking more data equals better tracking. However, too many columns can make the board **cluttered and difficult to navigate**.

- ♦ **How to Fix It:**

  - **Use only the essential columns** needed for your workflow.
  - Group similar data types using **Dropdown Columns** instead of multiple Status Columns.
  - Regularly **review and remove unused columns** to keep boards clean.

🔍 **Best Practice:**

- A simple project board should have:
  - ○ **Task Name** (Text)
  - ○ **Status** (To Do, In Progress, Done)
  - ○ **Due Date** (Date)
  - ○ **Assigned To** (People)
  - ○ **Priority** (Dropdown)

🚀 **Fixing this mistake makes boards easier to read and manage!**

---

2. Ignoring Automations and Doing Everything Manually

■ **The Mistake:**
Many users **don't leverage automation** and end up **managing repetitive tasks manually**, which wastes time.

- ♦ **How to Fix It:**

  - Use **Automations** to automatically move tasks, assign team members, and send reminders.
  - Create rules like:
    - ○ ■ "When Status changes to Done, move item to Completed group."
    - ○ ■ "If Priority is High, notify the Project Manager."
    - ○ ■ "When a due date arrives, notify the task owner."

📍 **Pro Tip:**
Explore **Monday.com's automation templates** to find time-saving workflows.

🚀 **Fixing this mistake eliminates repetitive work and streamlines processes.**

3. Not Using Groups to Structure Tasks Efficiently

■ The Mistake:
New users **dump all tasks into a single list**, making it hard to **prioritize, track, and organize** projects.

- ◆ How to Fix It:

  - Use **Groups** to **organize tasks by phase, team, or priority**.
  - Examples of effective group structures:
    - ○ **By Project Phases**: "Planning," "Execution," "Review," "Completed."
    - ○ **By Sprints**: "Sprint 1," "Sprint 2," "Sprint 3."
    - ○ **By Departments**: "Marketing," "Sales," "Product Development."

♥ Pro Tip:

- Color-code groups to **visually distinguish different stages of your workflow**.

✦ Fixing this mistake makes boards structured and easy to navigate!

---

4. Neglecting Status Updates and Task Comments

■ The Mistake:
Users often **fail to update task statuses or leave comments**, leading to **unclear task progress and miscommunication**.

- ◆ How to Fix It:

  - Train your team to **update task statuses immediately**.
  - Use **@mentions** in the Updates section to notify teammates.
  - Add **progress notes** in comments instead of using external chats or emails.

♥ Pro Tip:
Use **Monday.com's Activity Log** to track changes and ensure updates are being made.

✦ Fixing this mistake keeps everyone on the same page and improves team communication!

---

5. Forgetting to Assign Owners to Tasks

■ The Mistake:
Tasks **without owners often get ignored**, leading to **missed deadlines and confusion**.

- ◆ How to Fix It:

  - Always **assign a task owner** using the **People Column**.
  - Set up **Automations** like:
    - ○ ■ "When a task is created, assign it to the team lead."
    - ○ ■ "When a task is overdue, notify the assigned person."

♥ Pro Tip:
Use the **Workload View** to **balance assignments** and avoid overloading certain team members.

✦ Fixing this mistake ensures accountability and faster task completion!

6. Underutilizing Dashboards and Reports

■ **The Mistake:**
Many users **fail to leverage dashboards**, making it hard to **get an overview of project progress**.

◆ How to Fix It:

- Use **Dashboards** to track key project metrics.
- Add widgets for:
    - ○ ■ **Project Progress** (Status Overview)
    - ○ ■ **Team Workload** (Who is overloaded?)
    - ○ ■ **Upcoming Deadlines** (Tasks due soon)
    - ○ ■ **Performance Metrics** (Completed vs. Pending tasks)

♥ **Pro Tip:**
Set up **weekly automated reports** summarizing project progress.

🚀 **Fixing this mistake helps managers track work efficiently without micromanaging!**

7. Not Using Templates for Repetitive Workflows

■ **The Mistake:**
New users **manually recreate project boards from scratch**, which is **time-consuming and inconsistent**.

◆ How to Fix It:

- Use **Monday.com's pre-built templates** for common workflows.
- Save your **custom boards as templates** for future use.
- Examples of useful templates:
    - ○ ■ **Project Management Template**
    - ○ ■ **Marketing Campaign Template**
    - ○ ■ **Bug Tracking Template**

♥ **Pro Tip:**

- Create **department-specific templates** to standardize workflows across teams.

🚀 **Fixing this mistake reduces setup time and ensures consistency!**

8. Ignoring Integrations with Other Tools

■ **The Mistake:**
Many teams **manually transfer data** between Monday.com and other tools like Slack, Google Drive, or Zoom.

◆ How to Fix It:

- Integrate Monday.com with:
    - ○ ■ **Slack** (Get notifications for task updates).
    - ○ ■ **Google Drive/Dropbox** (Attach files directly to tasks).
    - ○ ■ **Zoom** (Schedule meetings from Monday.com).

○ ■ CRM tools like HubSpot/Salesforce.

💡 Pro Tip:
Use **Zapier** to automate connections between Monday.com and hundreds of other apps.

🚀 Fixing this mistake saves time and eliminates unnecessary manual work!

---

9. Not Defining Clear Workflows from the Start

■ The Mistake:
Many teams start using Monday.com **without defining a clear process**, leading to **disorganized boards and inefficiency**.

- **How to Fix It:**

  - Before setting up your board, define:
    - ○ ■ What project phases you need.
    - ○ ■ What columns are essential.
    - ○ ■ Who is responsible for each task.
  - Standardize workflows across teams.

💡 Pro Tip:
Use **Monday.com's onboarding checklist** to set up an efficient workflow.

🚀 Fixing this mistake ensures a smooth and structured workflow!

---

10. Failing to Train the Team Properly

■ The Mistake:
New users **struggle with Monday.com's features** because they haven't received proper training.

- **How to Fix It:**

  - Provide **onboarding sessions** for new team members.
  - Share **Monday.com's help center articles**.
  - Assign a **Monday.com "champion"** in each department to assist others.

💡 Pro Tip:
Schedule **monthly training refreshers** to ensure everyone is using the platform effectively.

🚀 Fixing this mistake helps teams use Monday.com efficiently and confidently!

Final Thoughts

Mistakes are part of learning, but knowing **what to avoid and how to fix it** will help you **unlock the full potential of Monday.com**.

Quick Recap of Common Mistakes & Fixes:

✗ Overcomplicating boards → ■ Use only essential columns
✗ Ignoring automations → ■ Automate repetitive tasks

✗ Poor task organization → ■ Use Groups to structure workflows
✗ Lack of task updates → ■ Use status updates and comments
✗ Unassigned tasks → ■ Assign task owners
✗ Underutilized dashboards → ■ Set up visual reports
✗ Recreating workflows manually → ■ Use templates
✗ Not using integrations → ■ Connect Monday.com with external tools
✗ No clear workflow process → ■ Standardize workflows
✗ Lack of team training → ■ Provide onboarding & ongoing training

Now that you know how to **avoid common pitfalls**, the next chapter explores **Scaling Workflows for Large Teams or Complex Projects**—so you can **take your Monday.com expertise to the next level!**

Scaling Workflows for Large Teams or Complex Projects

As organizations grow, so do their **projects and team structures**. Managing **large teams or complex projects** with multiple dependencies, stakeholders, and workflows requires **scalability, efficiency, and clarity**. Monday.com offers a **robust suite of features** designed to help businesses **scale operations without losing control or productivity**.

This chapter explores **best practices for scaling workflows** and **avoiding pitfalls** that can hinder large teams or complex project management.

1. Structuring Boards for Large Teams

■ **The Challenge:**
Managing multiple teams and projects without **losing track of tasks or creating confusion**.

◆ **Best Practices:**

- **Use separate boards for each team or department** instead of overcrowding a single board.
- Create **a high-level board** that summarizes key projects from different teams.
- Utilize **subitems** to **break down complex tasks into smaller, manageable steps**.
- Set up **permissions and access control** so only relevant teams can edit their respective boards.

💡 **Pro Tip:**
Use the **Board Connect feature** to **link multiple boards together** for seamless tracking across departments.

🚀 **Outcome:**
A well-structured board system prevents clutter and ensures **team-specific focus** while maintaining **a big-picture overview**.

2. Implementing Advanced Automations for Efficiency

■ **The Challenge:**
Large teams spend **too much time on manual task updates and tracking**.

◆ **Best Practices:**

- Automate repetitive actions using **"When this happens, do that"** rules.
- Examples of **scalable automations:**
  - ■ "When a task moves to 'In Progress,' notify the assigned team."
  - ■ "If a due date is missed, notify the project manager."
  - ■ "When a high-priority task is created, automatically assign a team lead."
- Use **dependency-based automations** to **trigger the next phase of a project automatically**.

💡 **Pro Tip:**

- Automate **status updates**, **task handovers**, and **workload balancing** to reduce human error.

🚀 **Outcome:**
Advanced automation **reduces manual intervention** and **improves efficiency at scale**.

3. Using Workload View to Balance Team Capacity

◼ **The Challenge:**
When managing large teams, **some employees get overwhelmed while others have too little work**.

* **Best Practices:**

  * Use the **Workload View** to **see each team member's assigned tasks and capacity**.
  * Adjust **task assignments** in real time to **prevent burnout or inefficiencies**.
  * Set up alerts when a **team member is assigned too many high-priority tasks**.
  * Use **time tracking** to analyze how long different tasks take and adjust workload distribution accordingly.

💡 **Pro Tip:**

  * **Color-code workload statuses** for better visualization of overworked vs. underutilized team members.

🚀 **Outcome:**
A balanced workload ensures **consistent productivity without overburdening employees**.

---

4. Managing Complex Dependencies with Gantt Charts

◼ **The Challenge:**
Large projects have **many interdependent tasks**, making it hard to **track progress efficiently**.

* **Best Practices:**

  * Use **Gantt Charts** to map out task dependencies.
  * Define clear **start and end dates** for every phase of the project.
  * Set up **automations that trigger dependent tasks** once prerequisites are completed.
  * Regularly **review and adjust project timelines** based on real-time progress.

💡 **Pro Tip:**

  * Use the **Timeline View** for better visualization of overlapping tasks and deadlines.

🚀 **Outcome:**
Gantt charts provide a **clear roadmap**, helping teams **stay on schedule** and **anticipate bottlenecks**.

---

5. Using Dashboards for Executive-Level Reporting

◼ **The Challenge:**
Executives and stakeholders **need a high-level view of progress** without going into granular details.

* **Best Practices:**

  * Create **custom dashboards** that display key metrics, including:
    * ◼ **Overall project progress**
    * ◼ **Pending vs. completed tasks**
    * ◼ **Team workload distribution**
    * ◼ **Upcoming deadlines and risk areas**

- Use **Widgets** to **display KPI indicators**, **budget tracking**, and **performance charts**.

💡 Pro Tip:

- Set up **automated reports** that send **weekly progress updates** to stakeholders.

🚀 Outcome:
Dashboards **improve transparency** and help decision-makers **stay informed without micromanaging**.

---

6. Standardizing Processes with Templates and Playbooks

■ The Challenge:
Large organizations often have **inconsistent processes** across different teams.

- **Best Practices:**

  - Develop **standardized project templates** to maintain uniformity.
  - Create **workflow playbooks** that outline:
    - ■ Best practices for using Monday.com
    - ■ Task assignment guidelines
    - ■ Reporting procedures
  - Ensure **all new projects follow a pre-approved structure**.

💡 Pro Tip:

- Share a **Master Template Library** that teams can duplicate and customize.

🚀 Outcome:
Standardized workflows **streamline onboarding**, reduce **setup time**, and **maintain consistency** across projects.

---

7. Setting Up Role-Based Access and Permissions

■ The Challenge:
As teams grow, **not everyone should have access to every board or sensitive data**.

- **Best Practices:**

  - Use **Role-Based Access Controls** (RBAC) to limit who can **view, edit, or manage boards**.
  - Set up **private boards for sensitive projects** while allowing general access for broader initiatives.
  - Define **Admin, Editor, and Viewer roles** for different team members.

💡 Pro Tip:

- Regularly **audit user permissions** to ensure the right people have the right access.

🚀 Outcome:
Stronger security and **less risk of accidental data modifications**.

---

8. Integrating Monday.com with External Tools for Seamless Workflows

■ The Challenge:
Large teams often use **multiple tools** that need **manual data transfer** between platforms.

- **Best Practices:**

  - **Integrate Monday.com** with:
    - ▪ **Slack** for real-time notifications.
    - ▪ **Google Drive/Dropbox** for document storage.
    - ▪ **CRM tools (HubSpot, Salesforce)** for seamless sales pipeline management.
    - ▪ **Zapier** to connect with thousands of apps.

Pro Tip:

- Automate **data syncing** across tools to **reduce duplication and human error**.

Outcome:
Smooth cross-platform functionality **eliminates manual updates and improves efficiency**.

---

9. Ensuring Scalability with API Customization

▪ **The Challenge:**
Off-the-shelf solutions may **not always fit unique enterprise needs**.

- **Best Practices:**

  - Leverage **Monday.com's API** to:
    - ▪ Create **custom workflows**.
    - ▪ Automate **data syncing** with external databases.
    - ▪ Develop **custom dashboards** for executive reporting.
  - Work with **developers to build tailored solutions** for unique business needs.

Pro Tip:

- Use the **API Playground** to test and deploy custom solutions.

Outcome:
Customized workflows **improve efficiency and adaptability** as your business scales.

By implementing these best practices, organizations can **increase efficiency, improve collaboration, and maintain clear visibility** across multiple projects.

Quick Recap of Best Practices for Scaling Workflows:

▪ **Structure Boards Efficiently** – Separate teams, use high-level boards, set permissions.
▪ **Leverage Automations** – Reduce manual work, automate repetitive tasks.
▪ **Balance Team Workload** – Use the Workload View for even task distribution.
▪ **Manage Dependencies with Gantt Charts** – Visualize timelines, set task dependencies.
▪ **Use Dashboards for Reporting** – Provide high-level insights for stakeholders.
▪ **Standardize Processes** – Create templates, enforce consistent workflows.
▪ **Set Up Role-Based Permissions** – Protect sensitive data, assign proper access levels.
▪ **Integrate with Other Tools** – Sync Slack, Google Drive, and CRM systems.
▪ **Customize with API Solutions** – Build unique workflows to meet business needs.

Now that you've learned how to **scale workflows**, the next chapter will cover **Security and Permissions: Protecting Your Data** —essential for managing confidential information and access control in large teams.

Security and Permissions: Protecting Your Data

In today's digital workspace, **data security and access control** are critical, especially when managing **large teams and complex projects**. Monday.com provides **robust security features** and **permission settings** to help **protect sensitive information, prevent unauthorized access, and maintain workflow integrity**.

This chapter will guide you through **best practices for managing security settings and permissions** to ensure **confidentiality, compliance, and efficient team collaboration**.

---

1. Understanding Security and Access Control in Monday.com

■ **The Challenge:**
Organizations need to balance **data accessibility with protection**, ensuring that **only the right people** have access to sensitive data.

- ◆ **Best Practices:**

  - Assign **clear roles and permissions** to control **who can view, edit, or manage boards and workspaces**.
  - Restrict access to **confidential data** by using **private boards** and **limited access settings**.
  - Implement **audit logs and activity tracking** to monitor **who is making changes to important data**.

💡 **Pro Tip:**
Use **multi-factor authentication (MFA)** to add an extra layer of protection to user accounts.

🚀 **Outcome:**
A well-structured **security framework** ensures that **sensitive data stays protected while teams remain productive**.

---

2. Setting Up Role-Based Permissions for Teams

■ **The Challenge:**
When working with large teams, **not everyone needs access to every project or feature**.

- ◆ **Best Practices:**

  - Assign team members one of the following **permission levels**:
    - ○ **Admin:** Full access to all features, including user management.
    - ○ **Member:** Access to shared boards and workspaces with some restrictions.
    - ○ **Viewer:** Read-only access, ideal for stakeholders or external collaborators.
    - ○ **Guest:** Limited access to specific boards for contractors or clients.
  - Use **workspace permissions** to define **who can create, edit, or delete boards and projects**.
  - Set up **time-limited access for temporary users** to prevent unnecessary long-term access.

💡 **Pro Tip:**
Regularly **review and update permissions** to prevent **unauthorized users from accessing outdated or irrelevant projects**.

🚀 **Outcome:**
A structured **role-based permission system** helps in **minimizing security risks while maintaining collaboration efficiency**.

---

3. Using Private, Shareable, and Public Boards Wisely

◼ **The Challenge:**
Different projects require different levels of **data visibility and confidentiality**.

- **Best Practices:**

  - **Private Boards:**
    - Use for **highly sensitive projects** (e.g., HR, finance, executive planning).
    - Only invited members can view and edit these boards.
  - **Shareable Boards:**
    - Use for **collaborating with external partners, freelancers, or clients**.
    - Provides controlled access while **restricting sensitive company data**.
  - **Public Boards:**
    - Use for **internal company-wide announcements or team knowledge-sharing**.
    - Accessible to all team members, **but can be set as view-only**.

💡 **Pro Tip:**
Convert a **Public Board to Private** when transitioning from **open collaboration to restricted access**.

🚀 **Outcome:**
Proper use of board types ensures **secure, structured, and organized collaboration**.

---

4. Enabling Two-Factor Authentication (2FA) for Extra Security

◼ **The Challenge:**
Single-password authentication leaves accounts vulnerable to **unauthorized access and breaches**.

- **Best Practices:**

  - Enforce **two-factor authentication (2FA)** for **all users** to **enhance login security**.
  - Use **email, authentication apps (Google Authenticator, Authy), or SMS** for 2FA codes.
  - Educate team members on **how to manage and recover their accounts securely**.

💡 **Pro Tip:**

  - Enable **Single Sign-On (SSO)** for enterprise-level security **when integrating with identity management platforms** (e.g., Okta, Google Workspace, Microsoft Azure).

🚀 **Outcome:**
2FA ensures **extra security for user accounts**, preventing **unauthorized access due to compromised passwords**.

---

5. Controlling File and Document Access

◼ **The Challenge:**
Files and documents stored in Monday.com should not be **accessible to unauthorized users**.

- **Best Practices:**

  - **Restrict file uploads** to prevent unauthorized file sharing.
  - Use **cloud integrations (Google Drive, Dropbox, OneDrive)** to manage document permissions **externally**.
  - Assign **file access based on roles** (e.g., only managers can view financial documents).
  - Use **version control** to **track document edits and changes**.

Pro Tip:
Set up **file expiration policies** for **sensitive documents** to prevent **long-term access risks**.

Outcome:
Secure file management ensures **data protection and controlled sharing within teams**.

---

6. Using Audit Logs for Monitoring User Activity

The Challenge:
Large teams and enterprises need to **track changes and user activities** to **maintain compliance**.

- **Best Practices:**

  - Enable **audit logs** to track **who accessed, modified, or deleted boards and tasks**.
  - Regularly review logs to **identify suspicious or unauthorized activities**.
  - Set up **automated alerts** for potential security threats (e.g., multiple failed login attempts).
  - Use **activity history** to **restore changes if incorrect modifications were made**.

Pro Tip:

  - Use Monday.com's **Enterprise Plan** for **advanced security monitoring and compliance tools**.

Outcome:
Audit logs help **prevent unauthorized activities** and **maintain an accountable workspace**.

---

7. Managing Third-Party Integrations Securely

The Challenge:
External app integrations can introduce **security vulnerabilities** if not **properly managed**.

- **Best Practices:**

  - Restrict **which users can install or connect third-party integrations**.
  - **Review and approve** third-party apps before granting them access to Monday.com.
  - Regularly **audit connected integrations** and remove unused or outdated ones.
  - Use **API access controls** to limit **how external systems interact with your data**.

Pro Tip:

  - Set up **OAuth 2.0-based authentication** for integrations to **enhance security**.

Outcome:
A controlled integration system **ensures data integrity and reduces the risk of external breaches**.

---

8. Handling Offboarding and User Access Revocation

■ **The Challenge:**
Former employees or contractors should **not retain access** to sensitive company data.

♦ **Best Practices:**

- Implement an **offboarding checklist** that includes:
  - ○ ■ Removing user access to boards.
  - ○ ■ Disabling logins for departing employees.
  - ○ ■ Reassigning tasks and responsibilities.
- Use **time-based access** for temporary staff and external partners.

💡 **Pro Tip:**

- Automate **user deactivation workflows** for efficient offboarding.

🚀 **Outcome:**
Proper user offboarding **prevents unauthorized access after employment ends**.

Final Thoughts

Securing your **Monday.com workspace** involves a mix of **proactive measures, structured permissions, and constant monitoring**. By implementing these best practices, project managers can **safeguard data, prevent breaches, and enhance productivity** while ensuring **smooth collaboration across teams**.

Quick Recap of Security Best Practices:

■ **Use Role-Based Permissions** – Assign Admin, Member, Viewer, and Guest roles appropriately.
■ **Choose the Right Board Type** – Use Private, Shareable, and Public Boards wisely.
■ **Enable Two-Factor Authentication (2FA)** – Add extra login security.
■ **Control File Access** – Manage document sharing and restrict sensitive data.
■ **Monitor Audit Logs** – Track user activity for compliance and security.
■ **Manage Integrations Carefully** – Control third-party app access.
■ **Handle Offboarding Securely** – Remove access for former employees.

Now that you've secured your Monday.com workspace, the next section explores **real-world applications through case studies**. Learn how companies successfully **implement Monday.com for Agile Project Management, Marketing Coordination, and Remote Team Collaboration.** 🚀

Section 9:
Case Studies and Real-World Applications

Case Study 1: Agile Project Management in Tech

Agile project management has revolutionized **software development and tech-driven industries** by **enhancing collaboration, flexibility, and rapid iteration cycles**. Many tech companies use **Monday.com** to implement Agile methodologies effectively, enabling **sprint planning, backlog management, and real-time collaboration**.

This case study explores how a **mid-sized software development company** adopted Monday.com to streamline its Agile processes, increase transparency, and improve **team efficiency**.

1. The Challenge: Managing Agile Workflows with Dispersed Teams

A **mid-sized SaaS company** with teams in multiple locations faced challenges in:

✔ **Tracking sprints and user stories across teams**
✔ **Ensuring clear visibility into task progress and blockers**
✔ **Managing daily stand-ups, sprint planning, and retrospectives remotely**
✔ **Integrating tools like Jira, Slack, and GitHub**

Traditional tools lacked the **real-time collaboration features** needed to **bridge the gap between development, QA, and product teams**. Monday.com provided a **centralized, Agile-friendly solution**.

2. Solution: Implementing Agile Workflows in Monday.com

- **Step 1: Sprint Planning & Backlog Management**

  - The team created an **Agile board** with columns representing **backlog, in progress, review, and done**.
  - **User stories and epics** were captured as **items**, categorized by priority.
  - **Sprint backlog items** were assigned to developers, with **due dates and dependencies**.

- **Step 2: Daily Stand-ups & Task Updates**

  - Using **Monday.com's Status Column**, developers updated progress daily.
  - Teams leveraged **Comments & @mentions** for instant communication.
  - A **Dashboard widget** displayed sprint velocity and burndown charts.

- **Step 3: Cross-Team Collaboration & Integrations**

  - **Slack and GitHub integrations** kept stakeholders informed in real time.
  - **Automations** notified team members when tasks moved stages (e.g., "Ready for Review").
  - QA used **Monday.com Forms** for bug tracking, ensuring seamless reporting.

- **Step 4: Sprint Retrospectives & Continuous Improvement**

- A **feedback board** captured insights from each sprint retrospective.
- **Pulse surveys** collected anonymous feedback on team dynamics.
- Teams used **Monday.com Docs** for documentation and knowledge sharing.

---

3. Key Results & Benefits Achieved

✔️ **Increased Sprint Velocity**: Tasks were completed **20% faster**, reducing sprint rollover.
✔️ **Improved Transparency**: Stakeholders tracked real-time progress via Dashboards.
✔️ **Better Communication**: Daily stand-ups were streamlined, reducing meeting time.
✔️ **Seamless Integration**: Automated workflows **connected development tools**, reducing manual work.

💡 **Pro Tip:**
Using **Monday.com's Workload View**, managers **balanced developer workloads**, preventing burnout.

---

4. Lessons Learned & Best Practices for Agile Teams

- **Keep boards simple but structured**: Avoid overcomplicated workflows.
- **Use Automations to reduce manual work**: Set up rules for sprint transitions.
- **Leverage Integrations**: Connect with Jira, GitHub, or Bitbucket for **end-to-end visibility**.
- **Monitor team workloads regularly**: Use Workload View to **avoid bottlenecks**.
- **Encourage feedback loops**: Create **continuous improvement** through retrospectives.

🚀 **Outcome:**
By implementing Monday.com for Agile project management, the SaaS company achieved **better collaboration, higher efficiency, and more predictable sprint cycles**.

Monday.com's **flexibility, automation, and real-time updates** make it an **ideal Agile project management tool**. The next case study explores how a **marketing team** used Monday.com for **campaign coordination and cross-functional collaboration**. 🌐

Case Study 2: Marketing Campaign Coordination

Marketing campaigns involve multiple moving parts—**content creation, social media scheduling, paid ads, email marketing, and analytics tracking**. Without a structured system, teams can struggle with **missed deadlines, disorganized assets, and ineffective communication**.

This case study explores how a **digital marketing agency** used **Monday.com** to streamline its campaign coordination, **increase efficiency, and improve cross-team collaboration**.

---

1. The Challenge: Fragmented Campaign Management

A **fast-growing digital marketing agency** faced challenges in:

✔ **Managing multiple campaigns across different clients**
✔ **Tracking content approvals and deadlines**
✔ **Ensuring smooth coordination between designers, copywriters, and ad specialists**
✔ **Measuring campaign performance in real time**

The team previously used **email threads, spreadsheets, and messaging apps**, which led to confusion, **delayed content approvals, and missed deadlines**.

---

2. Solution: Creating a Centralized Campaign Hub in Monday.com

* **Step 1: Setting Up a Marketing Campaign Board**

  * The agency created a **Monday.com board** with campaign phases: **Ideation, Content Creation, Approval, Publishing, and Analysis**.
  * **Custom columns** tracked content type (blog, ad, email, social post), assigned team members, and due dates.

* **Step 2: Assigning and Tracking Tasks**

  * **Task dependencies** were set up to ensure content was approved before publishing.
  * **Automations** moved items to the next phase upon completion.
  * Team members received **notifications** for new assignments and approvals.

* **Step 3: Managing Creative Assets and Approvals**

  * The **File Column** stored graphics, videos, and ad creatives for easy access.
  * The **Approval Column** allowed managers to approve or request edits with a click.
  * **Comments & Mentions** facilitated real-time feedback within tasks.

* **Step 4: Coordinating Paid Ads and Social Media**

  * The **Timeline View** tracked **ad campaign schedules** to prevent content overlap.
  * **Monday.com's Instagram, Facebook, and Google Ads integrations** synced scheduled posts with the platform.

* **Step 5: Monitoring Performance & Reporting**

  * A **dashboard** was created to track KPIs, such as engagement rates, conversions, and ROI.
  * Weekly reports were **automated** and sent to stakeholders via email.

3. Key Results & Benefits Achieved

✔ **Faster Content Approvals**: Reduced approval delays by **40%**, ensuring timely publishing.
✔ **Improved Collaboration**: Team members communicated directly within Monday.com, eliminating email chains.
✔ **Streamlined Task Management**: Campaigns were organized visually, reducing confusion and workload mismanagement.
✔ **Better Performance Insights**: Custom dashboards provided **real-time analytics** for faster decision-making.

💡 **Pro Tip:**
Using **Monday.com's Integrations**, the agency **automated repetitive tasks** like social media posting and performance tracking.

4. Lessons Learned & Best Practices for Marketing Teams

- **Use templates to streamline workflows**: Monday.com offers **pre-built marketing templates** for campaign tracking.
- **Set clear deadlines and approvals**: Automate task dependencies to **prevent bottlenecks**.
- **Leverage Integrations**: Connect with **HubSpot, Mailchimp, and Google Analytics** for **seamless marketing management**.
- **Visualize campaign schedules**: The **Timeline View** helps prevent content overlap and missed deadlines.
- **Analyze data regularly**: Use Dashboards to **track campaign success** and adjust strategies.

🚀 **Outcome:**
By adopting **Monday.com**, the agency gained **full control over its marketing workflows, improved campaign efficiency, and reduced content delays**.

Monday.com offers **a powerful solution for marketing teams** by centralizing content management, automating approvals, and integrating analytics tools. The next case study explores how **remote teams** leverage Monday.com for **global collaboration across time zones**. ⬤

Case Study 3: Remote Team Collaboration Across Time Zones

With the rise of **remote work**, teams across different time zones face unique challenges: **scheduling conflicts, miscommunication, and lack of visibility into ongoing tasks**. Managing a distributed team requires a **centralized, efficient workflow** that ensures collaboration remains seamless.

This case study explores how a **global consulting firm** used **Monday.com** to overcome time zone barriers and **enhance remote teamwork and productivity**.

1. The Challenge: Disjointed Collaboration Across Continents

The consulting firm had team members spread across **North America, Europe, and Asia**, each working in **different time zones**. They faced several key challenges:

✔ **Difficulty coordinating meetings and project timelines**
✔ **Delayed responses due to time zone gaps**
✔ **Lack of visibility into who was working on what**
✔ **Struggles with document version control and feedback tracking**

Previously, they relied on **email threads and messaging apps**, which caused **misaligned expectations and duplicated work**.

2. Solution: Creating a Remote-Friendly Workflow with Monday.com

- **Step 1: Setting Up a Global Project Dashboard**

  - The team **created a board** for ongoing projects with **real-time task tracking**.
  - Custom columns included: **Task Owner, Time Zone, Status, Due Date, and Last Updated**.

- **Step 2: Automating Task Handoffs Across Time Zones**

  - **Automations** assigned tasks based on time zone availability.
  - When one region finished work, an automation **notified the next time zone team**.
  - Updates were logged in the **Comments section** for full visibility.

- **Step 3: Managing Meetings & Availability**

  - A **Shared Calendar View** tracked availability across time zones.
  - The team used **Monday.com's integration with Google Calendar** to schedule meetings at optimal overlap hours.
  - **Asynchronous updates** reduced the need for real-time meetings.

- **Step 4: File Sharing & Real-Time Feedback**

  - The **File Column** stored documents, ensuring a **single source of truth**.
  - **Comment threads** enabled direct feedback without email chains.
  - **Version history tracking** prevented accidental overwrites.

- **Step 5: Performance Monitoring & Reporting**

  - A **custom dashboard** tracked key KPIs, task completion rates, and pending approvals.

- Weekly progress reports were **automatically generated and sent** to team leads.

---

3. Key Results & Benefits Achieved

✔ **Reduced Meeting Fatigue**: **40% fewer real-time meetings** by shifting to async communication.
✔ **Faster Project Turnarounds**: Time zone handoffs **enabled 24/7 project progress**.
✔ **Improved Task Visibility**: All team members could **see progress at a glance**.
✔ **Seamless Document Collaboration**: **No more version conflicts** or lost updates.

💡 **Pro Tip:**
Monday.com's timezone-based task assignment automation ensures work continues **even when some team members are offline**.

---

4. Lessons Learned & Best Practices for Remote Teams

- **Use a centralized project dashboard**: Monday.com boards **enhance task visibility** and prevent work duplication.
- **Automate task transitions**: Assign tasks dynamically based on **team availability across time zones**.
- **Optimize meeting schedules**: Use **Calendar View and Google Calendar integration** to find the best overlap.
- **Emphasize asynchronous collaboration**: Encourage teams to **comment on tasks** rather than rely on real-time meetings.
- **Track performance through dashboards**: Use reporting tools to **measure task progress and team efficiency**.

🚀 **Outcome:**
By leveraging **Monday.com**, the firm successfully **coordinated a remote team across 10+ time zones**, improved **work efficiency**, and ensured a **seamless global workflow**.

Monday.com **bridges the gap for remote teams** by offering **real-time tracking, automation, and seamless collaboration tools**. Whether managing international projects or daily workflows, it ensures **team alignment and productivity—no matter the location**.

Section 10:
Future-Proofing Your Skills

Staying Updated with Monday.com's New Features

Monday.com continuously evolves to meet the changing needs of project managers, teams, and organizations. With regular updates, new features, and integrations, staying informed ensures that you **maximize productivity, streamline collaboration, and leverage the latest tools**.

This chapter explores **the best ways to stay updated**, adopt **new features efficiently**, and ensure your team is always using **Monday.com to its full potential**.

---

1. Why Keeping Up with Updates Matters

New features in Monday.com often include:

- **Improved automations** to enhance workflow efficiency.
- **Enhanced integrations** with popular tools like Slack, Zoom, and Google Workspace.
- **New project views** such as advanced Gantt charts and workload management.
- **AI-powered insights** for smarter decision-making.
- **Security enhancements** for better data protection.

By staying updated, you can: ✔ **Improve workflow efficiency** with automation upgrades.
✔ **Enhance collaboration** through new communication tools.
✔ **Gain deeper insights** using newly introduced reporting dashboards.
✔ **Ensure security compliance** with the latest privacy features.

---

2. Best Ways to Stay Updated with Monday.com

To keep up with the latest features and updates, you can **leverage multiple resources**:

- **Monday.com Product Release Notes**

  - Available at **[Monday.com's Updates Page]** (https://monday.com/blog/updates/)
  - Regularly lists **new features, improvements, and bug fixes**.
  - Includes **how-to guides** for implementing new tools.

- **Monday.com Webinars & Training Sessions**

  - **Live product demo sessions** to showcase new functionalities.
  - On-demand training modules for **specific feature deep dives**.
  - Offered through **Monday.com Academy** for all user levels.

- **Monday.com Community & Forums**

  - Engage in discussions with **power users and product experts**.
  - **Get early access insights** into beta features.
  - Ask questions about **best practices and feature implementations**.

* **Social Media & Newsletters**

  - Follow **Monday.com's LinkedIn, Twitter, and YouTube** for update announcements.
  - Subscribe to their **weekly email newsletter** for curated insights.

* **Beta Testing Program**

  - Apply for early access to **test and provide feedback** on upcoming features.
  - Helps **shape the development** of new tools based on real-world use cases.

---

3. Implementing New Features in Your Workflow

Whenever a new feature is released, consider the following process to ensure **a smooth transition and adoption within your team**:

✔ **Step 1: Evaluate Relevance**

  - Does the new feature align with **your current project management needs**?
  - How can it **improve your team's efficiency**?

✔ **Step 2: Test in a Small Group**

  - Use a **sandbox board or test workspace** to **experiment with the feature**.
  - Gather feedback from a **pilot group** before full rollout.

✔ **Step 3: Train Your Team**

  - Organize an **internal walkthrough session**.
  - Use **Monday.com tutorials and documentation** for self-learning.

✔ **Step 4: Monitor Adoption and Optimize**

  - Track usage and engagement through **Dashboards**.
  - Adjust workflows if necessary to **fully integrate new capabilities**.

---

4. Notable Recent Monday.com Updates

While updates are frequent, here are **some key feature enhancements from the past year** that have significantly improved project management:

🚀 **Advanced Workload Management**

  - Enhanced **resource planning tools** to manage multiple projects.
  - Custom filters to **assign tasks dynamically based on capacity**.

📅 **Improved Calendar and Timeline Views**

  - Drag-and-drop functionality for **seamless schedule adjustments**.
  - **Color-coded tasks** for better visualization.

🔗 **Deeper Integrations with Third-Party Apps**

  - Native integrations for **Microsoft Teams, Zoom, and Salesforce**.
  - Real-time sync for **Google Calendar and Outlook**.

📽 Security & Compliance Enhancements

- **Enterprise-grade permissions** for better access control.
- Improved **audit logs for tracking changes**.

💡 AI-Powered Insights

- Smart automation recommendations based on **usage patterns**.
- AI-driven **task prioritization and workload balancing**.

Final Thoughts

Monday.com is a **constantly evolving platform**, and staying updated ensures that you **continue optimizing workflows, improving efficiency, and leveraging the latest innovations**. By using the resources outlined in this chapter, you can **keep your team ahead of the curve** and ensure long-term success with Monday.com.

✔ **Check for updates regularly**
✔ **Engage in training and community forums**
✔ **Adopt new features strategically**
✔ **Monitor performance and adjust workflows**

By proactively **staying informed and implementing new features**, you position your team for **greater efficiency and smoother project execution** in an ever-changing digital landscape.

Adapting to Evolving Project Management Trends

The **field of project management** is constantly evolving due to **technological advancements, shifting work dynamics, and new methodologies**. To stay ahead, project managers must be **agile, adaptable, and proactive** in embracing these changes.

This chapter explores the **key trends shaping project management**, how **Monday.com aligns with these trends**, and actionable strategies for **staying relevant in an ever-changing landscape**.

---

1. Key Trends in Project Management

Several **transformative trends** are reshaping the way projects are planned, executed, and managed. These include:

▩ The Rise of Hybrid and Remote Work

- Teams are increasingly **distributed across time zones**.
- Demand for **asynchronous collaboration tools** like Monday.com, Slack, and Zoom has surged.
- Monday.com's **real-time updates, automation, and integrations** help bridge communication gaps.

▩ AI and Automation in Project Management

- AI-powered project tools are **reducing manual workload**.
- Monday.com's **AI-powered insights and automation features** streamline repetitive tasks.
- **Predictive analytics** enhance **risk assessment and project forecasting**.

▩ Agile & Lean Methodologies

- Agile adoption is growing beyond IT and software development.
- Companies use **Kanban, Scrum, and Lean methodologies** to stay flexible.
- Monday.com's **custom workflows, sprint planning templates, and Agile boards** support this shift.

⬤ Sustainability and Ethical Project Management

- ESG (Environmental, Social, Governance) initiatives are becoming standard.
- Teams prioritize **eco-friendly project solutions and ethical business practices**.
- Monday.com's **reporting and analytics** help track sustainability metrics.

🔒 Increased Focus on Data Security & Compliance

- **GDPR, CCPA, and ISO 27001 compliance** impact project management tools.
- Organizations need **secure, cloud-based platforms** for collaboration.
- Monday.com ensures **data privacy through role-based permissions, encryption, and audit trails**.

---

2. How Monday.com Supports Modern Project Management Trends

Monday.com continuously **adapts to emerging trends** by rolling out **innovative features** that help project managers **stay competitive**.

Trend	Monday.com Solution
Hybrid & Remote Work	Cloud-based collaboration, task tracking, and integrations with Slack/Zoom.
AI & Automation	AI-driven automation, predictive task prioritization, and workflow optimization.
Agile & Lean	Agile templates, sprint tracking boards, and workflow customizations.
Sustainability & ESG	Data tracking dashboards for **measuring sustainability initiatives**.
Data Security & Compliance	Advanced **role-based permissions, encryption, and GDPR compliance**.

By leveraging Monday.com's **customizable workflows, automation, and AI-driven insights**, project managers can **adapt to trends efficiently**.

---

3. Strategies for Adapting to Industry Changes

To remain competitive in an evolving landscape, project managers must **adopt a proactive approach** to learning and implementing new methodologies.

✊ Continuous Learning & Professional Development

- Stay updated with **project management certifications (PMP, PMI-ACP, PRINCE2, etc.)**.
- Enroll in **Monday.com Academy** to explore advanced platform capabilities.
- Follow **thought leaders and industry blogs** for emerging trends.

💡 Embracing a Culture of Innovation

- **Test and iterate** new workflows instead of sticking to rigid structures.
- **Encourage team members** to suggest process improvements.
- Leverage Monday.com's **experimentation features**, like A/B testing boards.

🛠 Customizing Monday.com for Future Trends

- Build **custom dashboards** to track KPIs and emerging business metrics.
- Integrate with **AI-driven tools** for real-time insights.
- Use **Monday.com's API** for advanced workflow automation.

🧩 Integrating New Technologies

- Experiment with **machine learning-powered task automation**.
- Use **natural language processing (NLP) tools** to analyze team feedback.
- Incorporate **IoT (Internet of Things) data** for real-time project tracking.

---

4. Future-Proofing Your Project Management Career

As project management evolves, staying relevant requires **continuous learning, technological adaptability, and strategic planning**.

✔ Steps to Stay Ahead

◼ **Attend industry conferences and webinars** (e.g., PMI Global Conference, AgileSummit).
◼ **Join online communities and discussion forums** (Reddit, LinkedIn Groups, PM Stack Exchange).
◼ **Experiment with Monday.com's Beta Features** for early access to new tools.
◼ **Read case studies on industry best practices** for real-world insights.
◼ **Upskill through AI and data analytics training** to make data-driven decisions.

Final Thoughts

Adapting to **evolving project management trends** is **not optional—it's essential** for long-term success. By leveraging **Monday.com's flexible, future-proof tools**, project managers can **stay competitive, drive innovation, and lead with confidence** in the digital age.

✔ **Monitor industry trends and best practices.**
✔ **Adopt new technologies and integrate AI-driven tools.**
✔ **Leverage Monday.com's automation and analytics features.**
✔ **Invest in continuous learning and team training.**

By **staying informed, agile, and innovative**, project managers can successfully **navigate the future of project management with Monday.com** as their go-to platform.

Building a Monday.com-Centric Career Advantage

In today's **fast-evolving project management landscape**, proficiency in **Monday.com** is no longer just a skill—it's a **career advantage**. Organizations worldwide are shifting toward **cloud-based collaboration tools**, and professionals who can **leverage Monday.com effectively** are in high demand.

This chapter explores **how to position yourself as a Monday.com expert**, advance your career, and **become an indispensable asset** in any organization.

---

1. Why Monday.com Skills Are a Career Game-Changer

Monday.com has **transformed** the way teams **manage projects, automate workflows, and enhance productivity**. Mastering this platform can **significantly boost your career** by:

■ **Increasing job opportunities** – Many companies actively seek **Monday.com specialists**.
■ **Enhancing leadership skills** – Efficient **project management and team collaboration** make you a stronger leader.
■ **Boosting efficiency and productivity** – Advanced automation skills help **streamline workflows**, making you an asset.
■ **Positioning you as a technology-savvy professional** – Mastering modern project management tools **future-proofs** your career.

Who Benefits from Monday.com Expertise?

- **Project Managers** – Improve **workflow optimization and task automation**.
- **Team Leads** – Enhance **team collaboration and visibility**.
- **Freelancers & Consultants** – Offer **Monday.com consulting services**.
- **Business Owners** – Optimize **internal operations and project tracking**.
- **HR, Sales, and Marketing Professionals** – Automate **CRM, recruitment, and campaign workflows**.

---

2. How to Build Your Expertise in Monday.com

Becoming an **advanced Monday.com user** requires **structured learning, hands-on practice, and professional development**.

♠ Step 1: Learn the Fundamentals

- Complete **Monday.com's Academy courses** (available on their official site).
- Familiarize yourself with:
    - **Boards, Columns, and Workflows**.
    - **Automations and Integrations**.
    - **Dashboards and Reporting**.
- **Join Monday.com's Community** to stay updated on **best practices and feature updates**.

⚒ Step 2: Gain Hands-on Experience

- Create **dummy projects** to experiment with **different workflows**.
- Apply **Monday.com solutions** to your daily tasks.
- Optimize **existing project boards** for **efficiency and automation**.
- Work on **real-world projects** to solidify **practical knowledge**.

📌 Step 3: Get Certified in Monday.com

- Monday.com offers **certifications** that prove your expertise.
- Earning certifications can:
    - Strengthen **your resume and LinkedIn profile**.
    - Open doors to **higher-paying roles**.
    - Establish **credibility in the job market**.

📣 Step 4: Share Your Knowledge

- Start a **blog or YouTube channel** sharing Monday.com tips.
- Host **workshops** or **internal training sessions** at your company.
- Become an **active contributor** in **Monday.com's online community**.
- Publish **case studies** showcasing successful **workflow optimizations**.

---

3. Monetizing Your Monday.com Expertise

Once you have **advanced skills**, you can turn them into **income-generating opportunities**.

🚀 Career Advancement & Salary Growth

- Employees with **Monday.com expertise** often qualify for:
    - **Higher-paying project management roles**.
    - **Leadership positions** due to improved **team coordination skills**.
    - **Specialized consulting** for businesses needing workflow improvements.

■ Freelancing & Consulting

- Offer **Monday.com implementation, customization, and training services**.
- Charge for **custom workflow setup** and **automation strategies**.
- Help companies integrate **Monday.com with third-party tools (Slack, Google Drive, CRM platforms, etc.)**.

🏠 Teaching & Coaching

- Conduct **online training courses** on **Udemy, Teachable, or Coursera**.
- Create a **membership community** for **Monday.com enthusiasts**.
- Offer **corporate training sessions** to organizations adopting **Monday.com**.

---

4. Showcasing Your Monday.com Skills for Career Growth

To **maximize your career potential**, you must **effectively market your Monday.com skills**.

✔ Optimize Your LinkedIn Profile

- Highlight **Monday.com expertise** in your **headline and skills section**.
- Post **case studies or workflow optimizations** you've implemented.
- Connect with **Monday.com professionals and recruiters**.

■ Build a Monday.com-Centric Resume

- Emphasize **process improvements and automation** using Monday.com.
- Quantify achievements (e.g., "Reduced project turnaround time by **30%** using Monday.com's workflow automation").

- Include **certifications and training**.

🌐 **Network with Monday.com Professionals**

- Attend **Monday.com webinars and events**.
- Join **Slack or LinkedIn groups** dedicated to **Monday.com power users**.
- Engage in **community discussions and contribute solutions**.

---

5. The Future of Monday.com in Project Management Careers

As **Monday.com continues to expand**, businesses will **rely more on specialists** to **implement efficient workflows**.

Key Predictions: ■ **Increased demand for Monday.com specialists** in all industries.
■ **Higher salaries for certified experts** as organizations adopt **automation-first strategies**.
■ **Growth in Monday.com consulting services** for companies needing **custom workflow solutions**.
■ **Expansion of Monday.com integrations** with **AI, machine learning, and advanced reporting tools**.

By **investing in your Monday.com expertise today**, you **position yourself for long-term career success** in **project management, consulting, and beyond**.

Final Thoughts

Building a Monday.com-centric career advantage is about more than just learning the platform—it's about becoming **an expert in workflow automation, collaboration, and efficiency**.

✔ **Master Monday.com's tools and features**.
✔ **Gain hands-on experience and earn certifications**.
✔ **Monetize your expertise through freelancing and consulting**.
✔ **Market yourself effectively to secure high-paying roles**.
✔ **Stay updated on Monday.com's evolving capabilities**.

By **leveraging Monday.com as a career asset**, you **future-proof your skill set and open doors** to **exciting professional opportunities** in the digital workforce.

Appendices

Appendix A: Glossary of Monday.com Terms and Features

Understanding **Monday.com's terminology** is essential for maximizing its **functionality and efficiency**. This glossary provides **definitions and explanations** for key terms and features, helping you navigate Monday.com with ease.

📌 General Terms

1. Workspace

A **workspace** is a **high-level container** where all your **boards, dashboards, and projects** are organized. Large organizations often create **separate workspaces** for **different teams or departments**.

2. Board

A **board** is the **primary structure** for organizing and managing tasks. Think of it as a **digital whiteboard** where you track projects, workflows, and team collaboration.

3. Item

An **item** represents an **individual task, project, or data entry** within a board. It can have **custom fields** such as status, due dates, and assigned team members.

4. Group

A **group** is a **collection of items** within a board, often representing **different project phases, task categories**, or **sprints**.

5. Column

Columns are used to **customize your board** by adding different types of data fields such as **status, text, people, timeline, and numbers**.

6. Subitem

A **subitem** is a **task nested within an item**, allowing for better **task breakdowns** and **detailed tracking**.

7. Status Column

A **status column** is used to **track task progress** using customizable labels such as **"To Do," "In Progress,"** and **"Done."**

🛠 Key Features and Functions

8. Automations

Automations allow users to **automate repetitive tasks** (e.g., "When a task is marked as 'Done,' move it to the completed group").

9. Integrations

Monday.com integrates with tools like **Slack, Zoom, Google Drive, Microsoft Teams, and more**, enabling seamless workflows.

10. Dashboards

Dashboards **visualize project progress** through widgets like **charts, task lists, and workload views**.

11. Timeline View

Similar to a **Gantt chart**, the **Timeline View** helps track **task durations and dependencies**.

12. Workload View

The **Workload View** helps managers balance **team capacities** by showing **who is working on what and when**.

13. My Work

"My Work" provides a **personalized task view**, showing **tasks assigned to you** across all boards.

14. Forms

Forms convert input fields into **structured data** that automatically create new **items** in a board.

◼ Data and Reporting

15. Filters and Search

Filters allow you to **view specific tasks** based on **status, due dates, and assigned team members**.

16. Custom Fields

Custom fields allow users to **tailor boards** by adding specific **data types and fields**.

17. Permissions & Security

Monday.com provides **role-based access control**, letting **admins restrict access** to **boards, workspaces, and automations**.

18. Monday.com API

The Monday.com API allows developers to **integrate and customize workflows** with external applications.

◼ Collaboration and Teamwork

19. Comments & Updates

Users can leave **comments and updates** within tasks, ensuring **transparent communication**.

20. File Sharing

Attach and share **files, documents, and images** directly in **items and tasks**.

21. Notifications

Monday.com provides **real-time notifications** to keep users informed about **task updates, mentions, and deadlines**.

22. Time Tracking

The **time tracking column** allows team members to **log time spent** on specific tasks.

● Advanced Features

23. Monday Workdocs

A collaborative **document workspace** where teams can **brainstorm, draft, and document workflows** within Monday.com.

24. Pulse

A feature that provides **team health insights** by capturing feedback through **surveys and pulse check-ins**.

25. Templates

Pre-built board structures that help teams **set up workflows quickly**.

This **glossary serves as a quick reference** for anyone looking to **maximize their use of Monday.com**. Familiarizing yourself with these **core terms and features** will allow you to **navigate the platform effectively and optimize your project workflows**.

Appendix B: Quick Reference Guide for Keyboard Shortcuts

Monday.com offers a range of **keyboard shortcuts** to help project managers and teams **navigate, edit, and manage tasks efficiently**. This **quick reference guide** provides an overview of the **most useful shortcuts** to enhance your **workflow speed** and **boost productivity**.

📌 Navigation Shortcuts

Action	Shortcut
Open **Search bar**	Ctrl + B
Open **Quick Search**	/ (forward slash)
Move between **boards**	Ctrl + Shift + Arrow Keys
Navigate between **items**	Arrow Keys (Up/Down)
Open an **item card**	Enter

📋 Editing Shortcuts

Action	Shortcut
Edit an **item name**	Shift + Enter
Save changes and **exit editing mode**	Esc
Duplicate an **item**	Ctrl + D
Delete an **item**	Ctrl + Backspace
Add a **new item**	Shift + N

📋 Task & Board Management

Action	Shortcut
Expand or collapse **groups**	Ctrl + G
Assign a **task to a user**	@ + (username)
Change **status**	Click the **Status Column** and start typing
Open the **Automation Center**	Ctrl + Shift + A

◼ Viewing & Filtering Data

Action	Shortcut
Open **Filter menu**	F
Toggle **Full-Screen Mode**	F11
Show only **tasks assigned to you**	M
Toggle **Dark Mode** (if available)	Ctrl + Shift + D

◼ Collaboration & Communication

Action	Shortcut
Add a **comment** in an update	Ctrl + Shift + U
Mention a **team member**	@ + (username)
Add an **emoji reaction**	: + (emoji name)
Attach a **file** to a task	Ctrl + Shift + F

🚀 Productivity Boosters

Action	Shortcut
Open **Dashboard View**	Ctrl + Shift + D
Open **Timeline View**	Ctrl + Shift + T
Open **Workload View**	Ctrl + Shift + W
Open **Inbox**	Ctrl + Shift + I

🔗 Integration Shortcuts

Action	Shortcut
Sync with **Google Calendar**	Ctrl + Shift + C
Open **Integrations Panel**	Ctrl + Shift + I
Open **API & Developers Settings**	Ctrl + Shift + X

Mastering **Monday.com's keyboard shortcuts** can significantly **enhance your productivity** by reducing **manual clicks and navigation time**. Use this **Quick Reference Guide** to streamline your **workflow management and collaboration** within Monday.com.

Appendix C: Template Library for Common Project Types

Monday.com offers a wide range of **pre-built templates** that help project managers quickly set up their workflows. Whether you are managing software development, marketing campaigns, or sales pipelines, templates provide a **structured starting point** to optimize efficiency and collaboration.

This appendix provides a **library of common project templates**, describing their use cases and key features.

📌 1. Project Management Templates

1.1 Basic Project Management

Use Case: Suitable for general project tracking across various industries.
Key Features:

- **Task Tracking:** To-do lists, progress columns
- **Deadline Management:** Timeline and calendar views
- **Team Collaboration:** Assignments and updates

1.2 Agile Development Board

Use Case: Ideal for software development teams following Agile methodologies.
Key Features:

- **Sprint Planning:** Backlog, in-progress, completed tasks
- **Kanban View:** Drag-and-drop task management
- **Bug Tracking:** Custom columns for issue severity and priority

1.3 Product Roadmap

Use Case: Used by product managers to track feature development.
Key Features:

- **Phase-Based Planning:** Idea, development, testing, launch
- **Milestone Tracking:** Timelines and Gantt charts
- **Stakeholder Updates:** Status reporting dashboard

📣 2. Marketing & Sales Templates

2.1 Marketing Campaign Planner

Use Case: Organizing multi-channel marketing campaigns.
Key Features:

- **Content Calendar:** Social media posts, blog scheduling
- **Campaign Tracking:** Goals, KPIs, and budgets
- **Collaboration:** File attachments for graphics and copy

2.2 CRM & Sales Pipeline

Use Case: Tracking leads, deals, and customer relationships.
Key Features:

- **Lead Tracking:** Custom status columns for deal stages
- **Automations:** Email follow-ups and sales task reminders
- **Reporting Dashboard:** Monthly and quarterly revenue tracking

2.3 Event Planning

Use Case: Coordinating events, conferences, and virtual summits.
Key Features:

- **Task Assignments:** Organizers, sponsors, speakers
- **Budget & Expenses:** Cost estimates and approvals
- **Timeline View:** Key event milestones

⚙ 3. IT & Engineering Templates

3.1 IT Support Ticket System

Use Case: Managing internal or external IT service requests.
Key Features:

- **Ticket Prioritization:** Urgent, high, medium, low
- **Auto-Assignments:** Route tickets to appropriate support agents
- **Status Updates:** In-progress, resolved, escalated

3.2 Software Bug Tracking

Use Case: Monitoring software issues and fixes.
Key Features:

- **Severity Labels:** Critical, major, minor
- **Assigned Developers:** Who is fixing each bug
- **Testing & Deployment Stages:** Staging, QA, production

3.3 DevOps Workflow

Use Case: Coordinating development and operations teams.
Key Features:

- **CI/CD Pipeline Tracking:** Build, test, deploy
- **Incident Response:** Alert system for downtime reports
- **Performance Monitoring:** Integration with monitoring tools

---

▪ 4. HR & Operations Templates

4.1 Employee Onboarding

Use Case: Streamlining new hire integration.
Key Features:

- **Checklists:** Training, paperwork, IT setup
- **Deadline Tracking:** Due dates for each step
- **HR Feedback:** Notes and employee progress tracking

4.2 Remote Work Collaboration

Use Case: Managing distributed teams effectively.
Key Features:

- **Daily Standups:** Remote check-ins
- **Project Assignments:** Clear ownership and responsibilities
- **Time Tracking:** Log work hours and productivity metrics

4.3 Procurement & Inventory Management

Use Case: Tracking purchasing and stock levels.
Key Features:

- **Purchase Orders:** Vendor, cost, delivery dates
- **Stock Monitoring:** Low stock alerts
- **Approval Workflows:** Automate order approvals

5. Finance & Administration Templates

5.1 Budget Tracking

Use Case: Monitoring company expenses and revenue.
Key Features:

- **Expense Categories:** Fixed and variable costs
- **Income Sources:** Monthly revenue tracking
- **Budget vs. Actuals:** Real-time spending updates

5.2 Legal & Compliance

Use Case: Organizing contracts and compliance requirements.
Key Features:

- **Document Storage:** Contract files and agreements
- **Renewal Reminders:** Expiry date tracking
- **Approval Process:** Automated workflow for sign-offs

Templates save time by providing **ready-made structures** for different project types. With Monday.com's customization options, you can modify each template to fit your team's specific needs. Start with a **pre-built template** and adapt it to **enhance productivity** and **collaborate seamlessly** with your team!

Appendix D: Resources for Continued Learning

To stay ahead in project management and maximize the potential of **Monday.com**, continuous learning is key. This appendix provides a curated list of **official resources, online courses, communities, and books** to help you expand your knowledge and expertise.

📖 1. Official Monday.com Learning Resources

1.1 Monday.com Help Center

- **URL:** [support.monday.com] (https://support.monday.com/)
- **What You'll Find:**
  - Step-by-step guides on all Monday.com features
  - FAQs and troubleshooting tips
  - Best practices for workflow optimization

1.2 Monday.com Webinars & Live Training

- **URL:** [monday.com/webinars] (https://monday.com/webinars)
- **What You'll Find:**
  - Live training sessions hosted by Monday.com experts
  - Q&A opportunities to get direct answers
  - On-demand recordings of past sessions

1.3 Monday.com Community Forum

- **URL:** [community.monday.com] (https://community.monday.com/)
- **What You'll Find:**
  - User discussions on workflows, templates, and automation
  - Tips from other project managers and power users
  - Feature requests and official updates

🎓 2. Online Courses & Certifications

2.1 Monday.com Academy

- **URL:** [monday.com/academy] (https://monday.com/academy)
- **What You'll Find:**
  - Free courses covering beginner, intermediate, and advanced topics
  - Interactive modules with real-world examples
  - Certifications to enhance your project management skills

2.2 LinkedIn Learning

- **URL:** [linkedin.com/learning] (https://www.linkedin.com/learning/)
- **Relevant Courses:**
  - "Mastering Monday.com for Project Management"
  - "Agile Project Management with Monday.com"
  - "Collaboration & Productivity Tools for Remote Teams"

2.3 Udemy & Coursera

- **URLs:**
  - [Udemy: udemy.com] (https://www.udemy.com/)
  - [Coursera: coursera.org] (https://www.coursera.org/)
- **What You'll Find:**
  - Project management courses incorporating Monday.com
  - Agile, Scrum, and Kanban methodologies
  - Business automation and integrations

📣 3. Professional Communities & Forums

3.1 Reddit – r/mondaydotcom

- **URL:** [reddit.com/r/mondaydotcom] (https://www.reddit.com/r/mondaydotcom/)
- **What You'll Find:**
  - Discussions on new features and best practices
  - Troubleshooting help from experienced users
  - Creative use cases and workflow inspirations

3.2 LinkedIn Groups

- **Group Examples:**
  - *Monday.com Power Users & Experts*
  - *Agile Project Management with Monday.com*
- **What You'll Find:**
  - Networking with project managers using Monday.com
  - Industry-specific workflow discussions

3.3 Facebook & Discord Groups

- **Search for:** *Monday.com Users Group*
- **What You'll Find:**
  - Live discussions on automation and integrations
  - Community-driven workflow templates

📚 4. Recommended Books on Project Management & Productivity

4.1 Books on Monday.com & Workflow Management

- **"Monday.com User Guide"** – A deep dive into setting up efficient workflows.
- **"No-Code Project Management with Monday.com"** – Learn automation and integrations for efficiency.

4.2 Books on General Project Management

- **"The Lean Startup"** by Eric Ries – Best for iterative project management.
- **"Scrum: The Art of Doing Twice the Work in Half the Time"** by Jeff Sutherland – A must-read for Agile teams.
- **"Getting Things Done"** by David Allen – Boost productivity and workflow clarity.

🌑 5. Industry-Specific Learning Resources

5.1 Agile & Scrum

- **Scrum Alliance:** [scrumalliance.org] (https://www.scrumalliance.org/)
- **Agile Alliance:** [agilealliance.org] (https://www.agilealliance.org/)

5.2 Business Automation & No-Code Tools

- **Zapier Blog:** [zapier.com/blog]b(https://zapier.com/blog/)
- **Make (Integromat) Learning Hub:** [www.make.com] (https://www.make.com/)

5.3 Remote Work & Team Collaboration

- **Harvard Business Review – Remote Work Resources:** [hbr.org] (https://hbr.org/)
- **Trello Blog – Remote Collaboration Tips:** [blog.trello.com] (https://blog.trello.com/)

Leveraging these resources will help you stay ahead in **Monday.com mastery and project management excellence**. Keep learning, stay connected with the community, and continuously refine your workflows for **better efficiency and team collaboration**!

Conclusion

Throughout this book, we have explored how **Monday.com** empowers project managers to **streamline workflows, enhance collaboration, and drive project success**. From setting up your first project board to mastering automations and integrating external tools, you now have a **comprehensive understanding** of how to make the most of Monday.com in your project management journey.

Project management is not just about tracking tasks—it's about **ensuring clarity, fostering team synergy, and achieving business goals efficiently**. By leveraging Monday.com's customizable features, automation capabilities, and integrations, you can optimize your team's productivity and keep projects on track with ease.

Key Takeaways

As you move forward, keep these **core principles** in mind:

■ **Start with a solid foundation** – Set up boards, groups, and columns effectively to reflect your workflow.
■ **Use automation wisely** – Reduce repetitive tasks to free up time for more strategic work.
■ **Emphasize collaboration** – Use real-time updates, file sharing, and integrations to keep your team connected.
■ **Stay data-driven** – Use dashboards, workload views, and reports to make informed decisions.
■ **Keep learning** – Monday.com is constantly evolving, so staying updated with new features and best practices is crucial.

Next Steps

Now that you've mastered Monday.com, **how can you take your skills even further?** Here are some actionable steps:

- **Implement what you've learned:** Start optimizing your workflows by applying the techniques covered in this book.
- **Explore new integrations:** Experiment with CRM, cloud storage, and communication tool integrations to enhance team efficiency.
- **Join the community:** Engage with the **Monday.com Community Forum** or **LinkedIn Groups** to exchange ideas and get advice from other professionals.
- **Get certified:** Consider taking an official **Monday.com certification** to validate your expertise.
- **Train your team:** Share your knowledge to ensure everyone on your team is aligned and making the most of Monday.com's capabilities.

A Future-Proof Approach to Project Management

As the workplace evolves, **digital project management will continue to be a critical skill.** Monday.com provides the flexibility and scalability needed to **adapt to change and thrive in fast-paced environments.** Whether you are managing an Agile tech team, coordinating a marketing campaign, or leading remote teams across different time zones, **Monday.com equips you with the tools to stay ahead**.

By continually refining your workflows and staying informed about the platform's latest updates, **you position yourself as a leader in modern project management.** The journey doesn't end here—continue experimenting, learning, and growing to **achieve even greater success in your projects**.

Final Words

Thank you for taking the time to explore **Monday.com for Project Managers: Blueprint to Success**. I hope this guide serves as a **valuable resource** in your project management endeavors. Now, it's time to **take action**—start optimizing your workflows, collaborate effectively, and lead your projects with confidence.

Wishing you **success, efficiency, and innovation** in all your projects!

www.ingramcontent.com/pod-product-compliance
Lightning Source LLC
LaVergne TN
LVHW060122070326
832902LV00019B/3097